Investment, Capital Market Imperfections, and Uncertainty

Investment, Capital Market Imperfections, and Uncertainty

Theory and Empirical Results

Robert Lensink, Hong Bo and Elmer Sterken

University of Groningen
The Netherlands

Edward Elgar
Cheltenham, UK • Northampton, MA, USA

© Robert Lensink, Hong Bo, Elmer Sterken 2001

Published by
Edward Elgar Publishing Limited
Glensanda House
Montpellier Parade
Cheltenham
Glos GL50 1UA
UK

Edward Elgar Publishing, Inc.
136 West Street
Suite 202
Northampton
Massachusetts 01060
USA
JK

A catalogue record for this book
is available from the British Library

ISBN 1 84064 085 5

Printed and bound in Great Britain by MPG Books Ltd, Bodmin, Cornwall

Contents

List of Tables

Acknowledgements

This book is the result of joint efforts in the field of investment, financial market imperfections, and uncertainty, which the authors started at the Department of Economics of the University of Groningen. Many people stimulated our work and discussed previous results. We would like to thank especially Bob Chirinko, Simon Kuipers and Gerard Kuper for their remarks.

Richard Gigengack and Ingrid Hermes made a valuable contribution by correcting the full text. We are also indebted to Jan Jacobs and Jan-Egbert Sturm for their willingness to give us assistence with LATEX. Their efforts made it possible to meet the layout requirements.

Robert Lensink   Hong Bo   Elmer Sterken

1. Introduction

1.1 FIELD OF INTEREST

Both firm-specific and aggregate investment are central objects of study in economic theory. Investment plays a pivotal role in explaining persistent growth. Production growth depends on the growth rate of inputs and the improvement of the quality of inputs, apart from the growth rate of total factor productivity. Accumulation of capital and R&D as the main cause of improvement of the quality of inputs are the most important accountable sources of growth in developed countries. Investment is also important for the explanation of business cycles. About 90 per cent of the fluctuations of output are driven by investment behaviour, although investment barely exceeds 20 per cent of GDP.

Empirical models of investment are notoriously troublesome. For instance, in macroeconometric systems the private investment equations perform badly in terms of variance explained. But also on a microeconomic level it is hard to get a grip on the determinants of investment. The successful empirical determinants of investment are often variables that are not suggested by theoretical models. Liquidity is typically a variable that performs well although it should not according to the traditional investment models. On the other hand, the user cost of capital or Tobin's q is often found to be insignificant although many theoretical models emphasize its importance.

Investment is an old object of study in economics. Important contributions are given for instance by Fisher (1911) and Keynes (1936). There is even an old interest in financial variables explaining investment (see Tinbergen, 1939). But the influential work by Modigliani and Miller (1958) focused the attention of investment models on the asset side of the corporate balance sheet. Neoclassical investment models were developed in the 1960s (see Jorgenson, 1963) and extended to q models by Tobin (1969). But even these models did not provide a proper explanation of firm investment.

In the last decade new insights into investment theory centered around two themes: the effects of uncertainty on irreversible investment and the role of capital market imperfections.

Arrow (1968) addressed the impact of uncertainty on irreversible investment thirty years ago, while Bernanke (1983) is one of the early revivers. The main insight from this literature is that a firm, being uncertain about the future and

1

knowing that it might be hard to resell capital, may benefit from waiting. Waiting can be profitable since it reveals part of the uncertain future states. However, there are also costs of waiting in the form of lost returns on immediate investment. If the gains of waiting exceed the costs of waiting, there is an option value to postpone investment. The seminal recent contributions in this field are by Dixit and Pindyck (1994) in microeconomics and Trigeorgis (1996) in a firm-specific setting.

The second promising new group of investment theories deals with the impact of capital market imperfections on investment. If capital markets are perfect, the financial structure does not affect the costs of investing. However, capital market imperfections due to *e.g.* asymmetric information or agency problems probably cause a wedge between the costs of external and internal wealth. In such a situation firms prefer to finance investment by internal funds. The seminal paper in this line of research is the one by Fazzari, Hubbard and Petersen (1988a) and the review article by Hubbard (1998).

There is a vast amount of literature on both of these new lines of investment theory. However, with the exception of a few empirical studies (*e.g.* Scaramozzino, 1997, and Peeters, 1997), there are virtually no studies available that deal with both new groups of investment theories, let alone try explicitly to combine these two strands of literature. This book tries to partly fill this gap by presenting an extensive overview of both new types of investment theory.

1.2   OUTLINE

The first part of the book deals with investment and capital market imperfections. Chapter 2 reviews the theoretical literature. The aim is to identify the sources of capital market imperfections and to explain how they may affect investment. It is shown that corporate investment becomes sensitive to internal funds in the presence of capital market imperfections. First, the Modigliani-Miller proposition, which assumes perfect capital markets, will be explained. Next, the focus will be on different models of capital market imperfections, such as the contributions by Stiglitz and Weiss (1981), De Meza and Webb (1987), Myers and Majluf (1984), as well as the agency theory. Chapter 3 deals with empirical studies on investment and capital market imperfections. The main problem in the empirical literature is to determine to what extent capital market imperfections cause corporate investment to be sensitive to internal funds. Several classes of reduced form models will be discussed: the accelerator-type and q models, Euler equation models and VAR models. The empirical contributions confirm the importance of internal funds for firm investment. However, there are serious discussions about the relevance of many of the empirical studies. An up to date survey of this discussion will be presented.

The second part of the book deals with investment under uncertainty. Chapter 4 starts with a review of the orthodox studies on investment under uncertainty. The orthodox models assume that investments have to be made immediately: there is no possibility of delaying them. Attention is paid to both static models, without adjustment costs, and dynamic models with adjustment costs. In addition, it is explained what adjustment costs are and how they can be modelled. The chapter surveys three orthodox contributions to the investment under uncertainty literature: Hartman (1972), Abel (1983) and Stevens (1974)-Nickell (1978). It will be shown that investment by a competitive risk-neutral firm is positively affected by uncertainty as long as the marginal productivity of capital is a convex function of prices. Chapter 5 deals with the option approach to investment. In contrast to the orthodox investment models, the option approach to investment under uncertainty emphasizes that investment is irreversible and that there is a possibility of delaying the investment decision in order to obtain more information about the future. Attention will be paid to the contributions by McDonald and Siegel (1986), Bertola (1998), Caballero (1991), Abel *et al.* (1996) and Sarkar (2000). In contrast to the main conclusion of the orthodox models, the option approach to investment shows that an increase in uncertainty may have a negative effect on investment by a risk neutral firm. The main reason is that for irreversible investments an increase in uncertainty probably leads to an increase in the option value to wait and hence delays investment. Chapter 6 deals with empirical studies on the investment-uncertainty relationship by presenting an up to date overview of existing empirical studies. First, it is explained in detail which methods are used in the literature to measure uncertainty. A distinction is made between so-called *ex post* and *ex ante* approaches. Concerning the *ex ante* approaches, the following methods are used:

1. the variance of the normal distribution of the variable itself;
2. the variance of the unpredictable part of a stochastic process;
3. the variance from the geometric Brownian motion, and
4. the (General) AutoRegressive Conditional Heteroskedastic ((G)ARCH) model of volatility.

Ex ante methods derive the proxy for uncertainty from survey data. Next, an overview of empirical studies is presented. It appears that most empirical studies find a negative effect of an increase in uncertainty on firm investment.

Chapter 7 concludes with some suggestions for further research.

PART ONE

Capital Market Imperfections

2. Investment and Capital Market Imperfections: Theory

2.1 INTRODUCTION

Due to the limited success of existing econometric models in explaining corporate investment, considerable intellectual attention has recently been paid to improving the theory of investment. Different routes are followed in an attempt to come up with more convincing theoretical explanations of corporate investment behaviour. One branch of the profession emphasizes the importance of costly reversibility and uncertainty, while capital market imperfections are the core of analyses within another line of research. This chapter reviews the theoretical work on the relation between financial market imperfections and investment.

The aim of this chapter is to identify the sources of capital market imperfections and to explain how these capital market imperfections may affect investment. Section 2.2 discusses the Modigliani-Miller (MM) irrelevance theorem in the classical world. The MM propositions form a landmark in the literature on corporate finance and have contributed considerably to the theory of investment. The theory of MM refers to the invariance of the value of the firm for its capital structure. However, for the subject matter of this chapter, its main contribution is that it is the theoretical underpinning of the literature arguing that financial structure does not affect the investment decision. In the MM world internal funds and external funds are perfect substitutes. The main assumptions underlying the MM invariance theory, and hence also the separability of the finance and investment decision, are perfect and symmetric information. In the case where information is no longer fully and perfectly available for market participants, the capital structure affects the market value of the firm, so that financial variables may become important determinants of investment. Section 2.3 discusses the economics of imperfection by focusing on information economics and, related to this, agency theory. We review e.g. the contributions of Stiglitz-Weiss (1981) and Myers-Majluf (1984). A common feature of all capital market imperfections models is that they result in internal and external funds becoming imperfect substitutes. Section 2.3 identifies the sources of capital market imperfections. How these capital market imperfections may affect

7

investment is discussed in Section 2.4. Section 2.4 will show that the existence of capital market imperfections implies that corporate investment becomes sensitive to the availability of internal funds and that an increase in capital market imperfections negatively affects investment. Section 2.5 concludes this chapter.

2.2   THE NEOCLASSICAL WORLD: MODIGLIANI-MILLER

A company can finance its investment by issuing either equity or debt. However, the return characteristics of both types of finance are totally different. Equity represents ownership in a company. The equity holder receives an uncertain share of the future profit stream of the company. Debt represents a fixed payment to the lender. A debt contract has limited liability, implying that the debt is not fully repaid if the earnings of the firm are insufficient to cover the payments of the debt, *i.e.* if the firm goes bankrupt. Hence, the dividend flow must be non-negative. Due to the different return characteristics of both types of finance one would expect there to be an optimal level of the leverage ratio (debt to equity ratio), which would lead to a maximization of the value of the firm. Surprisingly, however, this is not necessarily the case in a neoclassical world, as was shown for the first time by Modigliani and Miller (1958).

Before explaining the main elements of the theory of Modigliani and Miller, some basic issues related to the neoclassical theory of finance will be discussed. Moreover, we will briefly refer to Fisher's theory of interest since this is one of the most important theories prior to MM.

2.2.1   Neoclassical Principles

In the modern neoclassical theory of finance three pillars are usually mentioned: *arbitrage, optimality*, and *equilibrium*. Arbitrage refers to the notion that the same good or asset has to have the same price in each period in absence of any restrictions, optimality refers to the fact that rational investors strive for optimal returns, and equilibrium relates to the neoclassical idea that markets are cleared by price adjustment at each moment in time. Usually, the Arrow-Debreu economy is seen as the ideal classical world. The Arrow-Debreu world is based on the paradigm of complete markets, implying that there are no restrictions on the amount of contracts people can enter into, and hence any type of risk can be insured. Each possible future state is covered by a so-called Arrow-Debreu security (or state security, state contingent claim).

In case markets are complete, present value prices of investment projects are well defined. In such a setting all shareholders are unanimous and agree that the firm should take the investment decision that maximizes the value of the firm. If markets are not complete, however, present-value prices are not unique: the market alone does not provide a well defined signal for the value of the investment.[1]

2.2.2 Fisher's Theory of Interest

Fisher's (1930) *Theory of Interest* gives the first classical result on finance and production in a one-good economy. Fisher presents a model of a sequence economy without uncertainty over a finite number of periods. There is a short-term bond in each period which enables agents to redistribute their income across time. Each agent is both a consumer and an entrepreneur and has access to a production set. Fisher's main result is known as the *Fisher Separation Theorem*. This theorem states that a firm should determine its production plan so as to maximize the present discounted value of its profit, which implies that the firm's objective function is independent of the preferences of the owner. Furthermore, the theorem implies that the production decision is independent of the financing decision.

2.2.3 The Modigliani and Miller Propositions

The first extension of Fisher's separation theorem to a setting with uncertainty is made by Modigliani and Miller (1958). They show that a firm's financial policy is irrelevant. More precisely, they prove that the market value of a firm depends only on its profit stream and is invariant to its capital structure. Their basic argument is that arbitrage precludes the market value of a firm to be altered by a change in a firm's financial policy when the profit flow is given. In the case where investors have the same financial opportunities as firms, investors can always undo the actions of firms on the financial markets. The following example, which closely follows the original 1958 article of Modigliani and Miller, explains matters.

Assume that there are two companies. Company 1 is an unleveraged firm that finances its expenditures only by common stock. Company 2, on the other hand, finances its expenditures by both common stock and debt. An investor, holding a fraction α of the total outstanding stock of shares (S_2) of company 2, receives a return of:

$$Y_2 = \alpha(X - rD_2) \tag{2.1}$$

where Y_2 is the return from the portfolio, X the expected return on the assets (expected profit before deduction of interest) owned by the company, r the interest rate on debt, and D the market value of debt of company 2. Assume now that the investor sells his shares in company 2, borrows an amount of money on his own account and buys from the proceeds shares of company 1. If the investor borrows an amount equal to αD_2, money available for company

1 shares equals: $s_1 = \alpha(S_2 + D_2)$. The return from this portfolio Y_1 is:

$$Y_1 = \frac{\alpha(S_2 + D_2)}{S_1}X - r\alpha D_2 = \alpha\frac{V_2}{V_1}X - r\alpha D_2 \qquad (2.2)$$

where S_1 is the total outstanding stock of company 1, $V_1 = S_1$ is the market value of company 1, and $V_2 = S_2 + D_2$ is the market value of company 2. Note that the expected returns X are assumed to be equal for both companies. By comparing the above equations for Y_1 and Y_2 it is obvious that Y_1 only exceeds Y_2 when $V_2 > V_1$. In this case, the investor makes a profit by selling shares of company 2 and buying shares of company 1, which would result in a decrease in S_2 and hence V_2 and an increase in S_1 and hence V_1. Arbitrage will thus lead to $V_1 = V_2$. More generally, this implies for any firm j in class k:

$$V_j = (S_j + D_j) = \frac{\overline{X}_j}{\rho_k} \qquad (2.3)$$

This is the famous proposition I of Modigliani and Miller. It states that "the market value of any firm is independent of its capital structure and is given by capitalizing its expected return at the rate ρ_k appropriate to its class" (Modigliani and Miller, 1958, p. 268). Sometimes this proposition is stated in terms of the average cost of capital, *i.e.* the ratio of the expected return to the market value of its securities. It then reads:

$$\frac{\overline{X}_j}{S_j + D_j} = \frac{\overline{X}_j}{V_j} = \rho_k \qquad (2.4)$$

Equation (2.4) shows that the average cost of capital equals the capitalization rate and does not depend on capital structure.

By defining the expected yield of a share in class j (i_j) as:

$$i_j = \frac{\overline{X}_j - rD_j}{S_j} \qquad (2.5)$$

and by using the equation for proposition I, it can easily be derived that:

$$i_j = \rho_k + (\rho_k - r)\frac{D_j}{S_j} \qquad (2.6)$$

This is Modigliani and Miller's proposition II. It shows that the expected returns on equity (yield of a share) equals the capitalization rate (and so the average cost of capital) plus a premium on the interest rate on bonds related to financial risk. Alternatively, the proposition shows that the average cost of capital, which equals the weighted average of the interest rate on bonds and the expected returns on equity, is not affected by an increase in the leverage rate. The decline in the average cost of capital by means of an increase in the leverage rate is exactly offset by the increase in the expected return on equity. Hence, if a firm substitutes cheaper debt for equity, the gains from cheaper debt will be exactly offset by an increase in the cost of equity which has become riskier as a result of the increase in a firm's leverage. For instance, assume that there are two firms with the same market value and equal profit flows. The firms differ in the sense that one firm is a leveraged firm while the other firm is unleveraged. It can then easily be shown that a change in the stream of profits has a much stronger effect on the percentage return per share of a leveraged firm compared to the percentage return of a share of an unleveraged firm. It is for this reason that equity holders ask a premium when the leverage rate increases.

The MM invariance proposition has been of great importance in the literature on corporate investment. Using MM theory as a theoretical underpinning, neoclassical investment theory (see Chapter 4), mainly associated with scholars like Jorgenson (see Jorgenson, 1963 and 1971), argues that financial variables, like cash flow, profits *etc.*, should not be included in investment equations. According to this theory, firms derive investment decisions by maximizing market value or equivalently optimizing profits, in a tax-free certain world with perfect capital markets. In this setting, the desired capital stock of firms, and hence also investment, only depends on factor prices and technology. The reason is simple: if financial policy does not affect market value, this implies that if firms want to maximize their market value financial variables do not matter. The real activity of the firm is then independent of its financing choice.

2.2.4   Assumptions Underlying the MM Propositions

For the development of corporate finance and investment theory the final MM propositions are not so important. A clear understanding of the underlying assumptions of the propositions, and therefore also the significance of the limitations, is more important, since it shows when finance matters and under which conditions financial factors are relevant in investment equations.

This section reviews the main discussions concerning the MM propositions. Due to restrictions in space, we will be as short as possible and concentrate on the main issues. One very important issue, especially for the purpose of this chapter, concerns the perfect information assumption. While this section will pay some attention to this issue, the next section will be entirely devoted to models based on the existence of imperfect information.

The discussions on the MM propositions can be centered around four issues:

1) firms can be grouped in risk classes; 2) bankruptcy is ignored; 3) there are incomplete markets and imperfect information, and 4) there are no taxes.

Risk classes
In the example Modigliani and Miller use to derive their Proposition I it is assumed that the expected returns X are equal for both companies. Modigliani and Miller (1958) justify the equality of expected returns for different companies by assuming that firms can be divided into similar risk classes or into a spanning set. In a risk class the uncertain underlying future cash flows of each individual firm would be perfectly correlated and therefore perfect substitutes. Initially the possibility of forming different risk classes was considered to be necessary to derive the MM propositions. However, Stiglitz (1969) proves that the MM theorem holds under more general conditions. By using a general equilibrium setting, he shows that the irrelevance of the financial structure for the market value of firms can be derived without making any assumption regarding risk classes.

Bankruptcy
Stiglitz (1969) shows that an important assumption underlying the MM propositions is the inexistence of bankruptcy. In their 1958 article Modigliani and Miller assume that bonds are entirely without risk, which implies that bondholders will always be repaid and that firms do not become bankrupt. However, in the case in which it is allowed to go bankrupt, bonds also become risky and the liability of equity holders will be limited. In such a situation, an increase in debt may increase the market value of firms.

Incomplete markets and imperfect information
The possibility of bankruptcy will, however, not invalidate the MM propositions if complete markets are assumed. The reason is that under the assumption of complete markets an individual can still replicate the exact patterns of returns even if a firm is allowed to go bankrupt. If markets are complete, bondholders may insure themselves against the risk of bankruptcy by borrowing and using the bonds as a collateral, so that in the case of default the bondholders only forfeit the security. On the other hand, when markets are incomplete and shareholders have limited liability, the financial structure does affect the market value of firms (see Magill and Quinzii, 1996, p. 405). Since shareholders make no effort to minimize losses in case of bankruptcy, they often choose a riskier production plan that generates more profit when it is successful, but less returns when it fails. Bondholders then often require a covenant to the long-term bonds issued by corporations. A *covenant* is a modification of the debt contract which may set limits to the future financial policy of the firm. Including covenants in long-term debt contracts is often in the *ex ante* interest of shareholders, since

covenants typically reduce the cost of issuing debt.

It should be noted, though, that the Modigliani-Miller propositions on capital structure irrelevance (Proposition I) and the corresponding yield requirements (Proposition II) in general do not need complete markets. The principle of no-arbitrage also holds in a general setting with incomplete markets (see Magill and Quinzii, 1996). Investors and firms are required to have access to financial markets.

One of the most important assumptions underlying the MM propositions is that individuals are not capital-constrained and have the same financial opportunities as firms, so that *homemade leverage* is possible. In practice this will not always be the case. Moreover, the MM propositions require all market participants to have full and equal information concerning the flow of returns (complete information markets), which is also in contrast to reality.

Taxes

Many of the discussions on the MM propositions deal with the effects of taxes – or more precisely with the effects of different taxation of debt and equity. Already in their 1958 article MM show that due to the fact that, unlike dividends, interest payments on debt are tax deductible, corporate taxation implies that the invariance condition not longer holds. Under plausible values for tax variables, an increase in leverage would increase the value of the firm. Modigliani and Miller (1963) show that this effect is even stronger, by pointing out that their 1958 article incorrectly assumed that the flow of annual tax saving should be capitalized by a capitalization rate for the relevant risk class. The annual tax savings, being a *sure* stream should be capitalized by the riskless interest rate, implying a more substantial effect of an increase in leverage on the market value of the firm. This article even suggests that the optimal outcome would consist of 100 per cent debt financing, which is clearly refuted by the data. Modigliani (1982, 1988) again reassesses the effects of taxation on the market value of the firm by rejecting the corrections made in Modigliani and Miller (1963), which results in an outcome that is very much in line with the 1958 article. Due to its large institutional details, however, it is beyond the scope of this chapter to present an overall and complete discussion of the effects of taxation on the market value of firms. It is preferable to consult comparative empirical work in this area (for instance, Rajan and Zingales, 1996). This discussion is concluded by stating that the introduction of taxation is an important factor that invalidates the invariance proposition of MM. However, it should also be noted that attempts to introduce taxes in the MM framework almost always gave results that do not seem to be in line with reality.

2.3 ECONOMICS OF IMPERFECTION

In a neoclassical world it is assumed that agents have full information on the characteristics of goods and services. However, in practice there will often be a situation of asymmetric information. Asymmetric information refers to a situation in which one agent has better information on the characteristics of a good or an investment project than another agent. While the problem of asymmetric information can arise in all kinds of markets, it is especially important to credit relationships. For instance, a manager of a firm often has more information on the characteristics of a project than a bank does.

Asymmetric information can lead to two problems. The first one is *adverse selection*, which refers to a situation where one agent has prior information on the quality of a good, whereas a second agent at most knows the probability distribution function. In a seminal paper, Akerlof (1970), provided the first rigorous analysis of the problem of *adverse selection* by analysing the working of a second-hand car market. He shows that in the case where sellers have more knowledge of the quality of the good or service sold than the buyer, a price adjustment for all goods may occur. Eventually a situation with no trade may result. This is the so-called *lemon principle* (see Akerlof, 1970).

Suppose that there are two categories of sellers in the market. The first category sells goods with a high quality, while the second category sells low quality products. The buyer cannot distinguish between the two groups and bids a price at which both groups are willing to sell. By lowering the price the sellers of the good product will no longer supply the good, while the sellers of the bad product will offer their product anyway. This splits the group: *i.e. adverse selection*. Hence, if the buyer is unable to distinguish between good and bad products, the price of the goods will drop, as bad products will drive out the good ones. In credit markets adverse selection refers to a situation where a rise in the interest rate may lead to a less favourable composition of the group of loan applicants. This may happen because borrowers who are prepared to pay higher interest rates are usually risk lovers, so that they undertake projects that are characterized by higher expected profits combined with a high probability of failure. On the other hand, borrowers with the highest probability of success may decide not to undertake their project after an increase in the lending rate. Hence, more risk averse borrowers may drop out of the pool of loan applicants when the lender increases the interest rate.

A lot of research has been conducted on the way in which markets try to cope with adverse selection problems. Two lines of research can be distinguished (see Mattesini, 1993, p. 28). The first group points at the crucial role of *signals*. Sellers of the highest quality goods may want to signal the quality of their product to potential buyers. If they need to attribute a certain variable to the good this leads to signalling costs. The attribute then is the signal. This leads to a distinction between informed and uninformed buyers. A well known example of a signalling model has been given by Leland and Pyle (1977). They show that entrepreneurs can signal the quality of their projects by financing the investment project with their own wealth. They argue as follows. Risk averse entrepreneurs may prefer to issue equity, even if they have enough wealth of their own. However, due to imperfect information the price of equity will be the same for bad and good projects. For investors endowed with good projects the equity price may be too low to make it interesting for them to issue equity and therefore they prefer self-finance. For entrepreneurs with bad projects issuing equity may still be preferred above self-financing. This behaviour may signal to the outside investor that those entrepreneurs financing their projects with wealth of their own are endowed with good projects. Hence, in this type of model the firm's choice of capital structure signals information of insiders to outsiders. The other line of research relates to situations where signals cannot provide more information on the quality of products. In that case, the price of a good is the only source of information concerning quality. This may lead to trade occuring at non-market clearing Walrasian prices.

The second problem related to asymmetric information is *moral hazard*. In the literature it is also known as *adverse incentive* or as the *principal-agent* problem. Moral hazard refers to a situation where two parties agree on a contract, but that one party afterwards takes an action that is not observed by the other agent. The *hidden actions* are meant to increase the welfare of the informed agent at the expense of the uninformed agent.

Information asymmetries between buyers and sellers may lead to so-called *equilibrium rationing*. Equilibrium credit rationing refers to the situation where a borrower's demand for credit is turned down, even if this borrower is willing to pay all the price and non-price elements of the loan contract. Unlike disequilibrium rationing, equilibrium rationing assumes that the price mechanism works. Rationing occurs after full adjustment of the price, whereas in disequilibrium rationing there is slow or no adjustment of the price. Especially in credit markets asymmetric information and thus *equilibrium rationing* is an important issue.

In the literature two types of credit rationing are distinguished (Keeton, 1979):

- *Type 1 credit rationing* refers to the situation where an agent cannot borrow the amount he wants to borrow at the existing interest rate. In this situation entire groups of identical loan applicants are entirely or partly excluded from borrowing. The bank is unwilling to lend to these groups. This type of rationing is sometimes called *redlining*. For example, if from a group of N borrowers all borrowers demand 1, and the total supply would be $N/2$, type 1 credit rationing would imply that each borrower obtains 1/2 unit.

- *Type 2 credit rationing* occurs when borrowers from an identical group are able to borrow whereas others are not. Using the above example, type 2 credit rationing would occur if some of the borrowers of the group obtain one unit, whereas others do not obtain anything.

There are two types of models that show that asymmetric information leads to sub-optimal investment. The first group shows that asymmetric information leads to underinvestment compared to the social optimum. The model of Stiglitz and Weiss (1981) is the basic reference. Another line of literature emphasizes that asymmetric information may result in overinvestment compared to the social optimum. The De Meza and Webb (1987) model is mostly associated with this group of literature. The next subsection deals with the basic insights of the Stiglitz and Weiss model. However, we will also pay some attention to the De Meza and Webb analysis.

The Stiglitz and Weiss model provides an explanation of credit rationing in the loan market based on information asymmetries. There are also models that explicitly deal with the equity market. The basic reference here is the Myers and Majluf model, which will be explained in Section 2.3.2 (see also Greenwald *et al.*, 1984). Finally, the agency theory will be discussed, the principal source being Jensen and Meckling (1976).

2.3.1 The Stiglitz-Weiss Model

The first paper in which the information asymmetry approach to credit rationing is introduced is by Jaffee and Russell (1976). They argue that if loans are priced at a single rate, both good and bad borrowers will be attracted. Jaffee and Russell show that banks can improve their profit stream by deliberately setting the loan rate at a level that differs from the equilibrium competitive interest rate since this may lead to an increase in the number of good borrowers.

The Stiglitz-Weiss model (1981) is an extension of the earlier model of Jaffee and Russell. The main message of the Stiglitz-Weiss model is that asymmetric information may lead to a situation where, among observationally identical loan applicants, some will get loans whereas others are denied (type 2 credit rationing). The model assumes that there is a pool of loan applicants who have projects with the same expected returns, but for whom the probability of success (P_i) and the return in case the project is successful (R_i^s) differ. P_i is the riskiness parameter. A decrease in P_i means greater risk in the sense of mean preserving spread (Rothschild and Stiglitz, 1970; see also Appendix B). Banks know that projects differ in riskiness but are unable to observe which projects are risky and which are not. Hence, a bank cannot discriminate among firms and therefore offers the same debt contract to all. Due to limited liability, profits of firms are zero for low returns and increase linearly for returns above a certain level. Hence, profits are a convex function of returns. Since the profit function is convex, Jensen's inequality (see the Appendix B) shows that the expected value of profits increases with the risk level. This implies that from a pool of borrowers with the same expected returns, the more risky borrowers generate the largest profits. Alternatively, this implies that the loan rate for which firm profits are zero (the reservation rate) is the lowest for the firm with the lowest risk project, so that the low risk firms drop out of the pool of loan applicants if a bank increases the loan rate.

Bank profits depend on the state of the world. In the case where the project of the firm is successful, the firm does not default and the bank gets the principal plus interest on the loan. However, in the bad state the bank only gets the return of the firm, possibly extended with collateral. The profit of the bank is linearly increasing for low project returns, whereas it remains constant above a certain level. Hence, the profit function for banks is concave in firm returns. For this reason, the project with the lowest risk generates the highest return for banks.

An increase in the lending rate has two effects on bank returns. It increases the average rate of return for banks since they get more interest on the loan. However, when the loan rate of the banks exceeds the reservation rate of the borrower with the lowest risk, this applicant will drop out of the loan market and negatively affect the return of banks. If the negative effect offsets the positive effect the average rate of return for banks declines. The model by Stiglitz and Weiss assumes that for low lending rates the positive effect exceeds the negative effect. However, beyond a certain threshold lending rate the negative effect will dominate. In this situation the optimal policy for the bank is to ration credit and not to raise the interest rate. The interest rate serves as a *screening device*.

Assume that a project of firm i has only two outcomes, a return of R_i^s in case of success and a return of R^f in the case of failure; the condition of equal expected returns for all firms implies:

$$P_i R_i^s + (1 - P_i) R^f = A \tag{2.7}$$

where A is a constant. Equation (2.7) implies that $\frac{dR_i^s}{dP_i} < 0$. Firms undertake the project if their expected profits exceed opportunity costs, which are assumed to be equal to a safe rate of interest σ times firm wealth W. All firms are assumed to have the same amount of wealth. Moreover, the project size and the firm's loan demand are equal. The above assumptions imply that a firm enters the market if:

$$P_i(R_i^s - (1 + r)B) \geq (1 + \sigma)W \tag{2.8}$$

where r is the interest rate charged by the bank. Substitute R^s from the equation for the same expected returns in the above equation. This gives:

$$A - R_f + P_i(R_f - (1+r)B) \geq (1+\sigma)W \qquad (2.9)$$

Since it is assumed that $(1+r)B > R_f$, the left hand side of the equation decreases in P_i. Hence, the above inequality holds as an equality for the firm with the highest probability of success, *i.e.* the firm with the lowest risk. In other words, the least risky firm has the lowest *reservation rate*. This implies that in case the bank increases the interest rate, the firm with the lowest risk drops from the pool of loan applicants since for this firm the bank lending rate exceeds the reservation rate.

In the models we have explained thus far, adverse selection is the main reason why an increase in the loan rate may negatively affect bank profits. However, Stiglitz and Weiss (1981) also analyse *moral hazard* effects of changes in the loan rate. In this case the change in the loan rate affects the behaviour of the borrower. Increasing the interest rate increases the relative attractiveness of riskier projects, for which the return for the bank may be lower. Hence, raising the interest rate may lead borrowers to take actions that are contrary to the interest of the lender. This provides another incentive for the bank to ration credit instead of raising the interest rate in a situation of excess demand for loans.

Some extensions of the Stiglitz-Weiss model
Several papers point out shortcomings of the original Stiglitz-Weiss model. Mattesini (1993, p.37) distinguishes four groups of criticism.

1. The debt contract is taken as given

Stiglitz and Weiss do not derive the debt contract from an optimal contractual arrangement. The debt contract is assumed to be given, and by assuming that a bank exists they abstract from the possibility that endogenous intermediary coalitions emerge. These endogenous intermediary coalitions evaluate loan projects *ex ante*, so that incentives of firms are structured in such a way that a Pareto-optimal allocation is brought about, which is not the case in the Stiglitz-Weiss model. Therefore, many authors have tried to assess the consequences of asymmetric information in the credit market by using a model in which a microeconomic justification of the debt contract is given, and in which intermediary coalitions emerge endogenously. Important examples are Gale and Hellwig (1985), Williamson (1986, 1987), and Boyd and Prescott (1986).

Some of these models try to explain why an optimal contractual arrangement in the credit market needs the existence of financial intermediaries, like commercial banks. We provide a short survey of one of the seminal models in this field: the model of Diamond and Dybvig (1983).

The Diamond-Dybvig model shows that in a world where private behaviour is not publicly observable, commercial banks are needed to provide liquidity insurance to reach a Pareto superior allocation as compared to the competitive outcome. In other words, in a world with imperfect information banks arise in order to improve risk sharing. The risk, which is modelled as a random need to consume early, is dealt with by the bank by providing liquidity. Thus, Diamond and Dybvig emphasize the bank's role in liquidity creation.

The Diamond-Dybvig model is about a world in which investing in illiquid assets is more profitable than investing in liquid assets. Two types of agents are considered (we use the terminology by Mattesini, 1993): patient agents who do not need liquidity in the short run (period 1), and impatient agents who need liquidity before the illiquid asset is liquidated (period 2). In period 0 all agents receive an endowment, which can be invested in a certain technology or privately stored. At this moment in time, an agent does not know yet whether he will be a patient or an impatient agent. This implies that market participants face uncertain liquidity needs. In period 1 each agent knows whether he belongs to the group of patient or impatient agents. In the case where this information would become publicly available, *i.e.* when in period 1 everybody knows who is a patient and who is an impatient agent, agents would in principle be able to decide on an *ex ante* (as of period 0) insurance contract in which it is agreed that agents who turn out to be impatient in period 1 obtain a certain amount of goods, and agents who turn out to be patient will obtain the rest. The Diamond-Dybvig model (1983) shows that the optimal *insurance* contract implies that agents, who turn out to be patient, are willing to give up some goods in order to increase consumption possibilities for agents who turn out to be impatient. In other words, the optimal contract implies that agents are buying insurance against the risk of being illiquid. However, if it is not publicly observable which type a particular agent is, *i.e.* every agent knows which type he is but has no information on the other agents, the optimal insurance contract cannot be implemented since nobody knows on what to base the insurance payments. Hence, if information is only available privately, liquidity insurance cannot be provided by competitive markets. The role of commercial banks in Diamond and Dybvig (1983) is to provide liquidity insurance when private behaviour is not publicly observable. Commercial banks are able to transform illiquid assets into more liquid liabilities by offering agents deposits. The commercial bank knows the amount of patient and impatient depositors. Using this information, commercial banks decide which part of their assets has to be liquidated in period 1 in order to be able to cover the optimal amount of withdrawals in this period and to maximize utility of the individual agents. This first-best allocation depends crucially on patient agents not withdrawing funds in period 1. However, if for some reason patient agents decide to withdraw funds in period 1, the bank will not be able to meet total demand for funds in period 1 and consequently also not in period 2. If patient agents believe that other patient agents will start withdrawing funds in period 1, it is better for all patient agents to withdraw funds in period 1. In this case the result will be a bank run, simply caused by a *sunspot*. Hence, the model has multiple equilibria, one of which is characterized by panic and bank runs. A crucial role in generating these bank runs is played by the *sequential service constraint* (first-come, first-served rule). Due to the *sequential service constraint* agents who actually prefer late consumption but fear early withdrawal of other patient agents, will decide to withdraw early. The bank run is assumed to be highly disruptive, so that it provides a strong justification for deposit insurance, since deposit insurance may eliminate depositors' panic.

2. No role for other instruments than the lending rate

In the 1981 model of Stiglitz and Weiss the lending rate is the main instrument of commercial banks. There is no role for other non-price instruments which may be used simultaneously with the rate of interest to induce self-selection among borrowers and hence may be used to solve the adverse selection problem. How does the model change if there are such instruments?

The basic idea is that banks may try to attract signals from the borrowers and induce loan applicants to engage in self-selection so that the debt contract will only be applied to borrowers for whom the contract is meant. A basic reference for this kind of models is Bester (1985). He shows that in equilibrium no borrower is denied credit if banks compete by choosing collateral requirements and the rate of interest simultaneously instead of separately, as is the case in the Stiglitz-Weiss model. In Bester's model, the equilibrium is characterized by separation of borrowers of different risk. Borrowers with high probability of default choose a contract with a higher interest rate and a lower collateral than borrowers with low probability of default. Hence, in contrast to the Stiglitz-Weiss model which is characterized by a credit-rationing equilibrium in which good and bad risks are pooled, the Bester model implies a separating equilibrium with no credit rationing.

3. Asymmetric information may also lead to overinvestment

A basic result of the Stiglitz-Weiss (1981) model is that projects with expected returns that exceed opportunity costs may lack funding. Hence, the model shows that due to asymmetric information underinvestment relative to the social optimum may occur. De Meza and Webb (1987), using a model similar to that of Stiglitz and Weiss, show that asymmetric information may also result in overinvestment. The main difference between the model of De Meza and Webb and that of Stiglitz and Weiss concerns the assumption with respect to the heterogeneity of projects. Stiglitz and Weiss assume that the expected returns of different projects are the same, while the probability of success and the return in the good state differs. On the other hand, De Meza and Webb assume that the return in the good state and the probability of success differs, whereas the expected rate of return of projects differs. The following description, which follows Lyon (1992), clarifies this. Assume that a project has a good and a bad outcome. Also, assume that firms have the possibility to put their wealth in a safe asset. Then, using the same variables as in the description of the Stiglitz-Weiss model, a project will only be undertaken if the following condition holds:

$$P_i(R^s - (1+r)B) \geq (1+\sigma)W \tag{2.10}$$

Since, in contrast to the Stiglitz-Weiss model, it is not assumed that all projects have the same expected return, a change in the riskiness of the project (P_i) does not affect the return in the good state (R^s). This implies that the above condition holds as an equality for the project with the lowest P_i. Hence, projects with the lowest risk are the marginal projects. For the marginal project, with a probability of success of P', the following condition holds:

$$P'(R^s - (1+r)B) = (1+\sigma)W \tag{2.11}$$

It is furthermore assumed that the banking sector is competitive, so that banking profits are zero in equilibrium. This implies that if banks gain some profits on low risk projects, they must lose on high risk projects. Thus, for the marginal project the costs of funds for banks will exceed the return:

$$P'(1+r)B + (1-P')R^f < (1+\sigma)B \tag{2.12}$$

By summing the above two equations, and by taking into account that $W + B = K$, where K is the capital stock, it follows that:

$$P'R^s + (1-P')R^f < (1+\sigma)K \tag{2.13}$$

For a social optimum all projects with expected returns greater than the opportunity costs should be undertaken:

$$P'R^s + (1 - P')R^f \geq (1 + \sigma)K \qquad (2.14)$$

Thus, for the marginal project the expected return is less than the opportunity costs and hence asymmetric information leads to overinvestment relative to the social optimum. The reason is that firms do not bother about the return of the project in states of default so that poor investment are undertaken.

The De Meza and Webb model has important consequences for a change in wealth on the equilibrium level of investment. It can be shown easily that the effect differs for low risk firms and the marginal firm. For low risk firms an increase in wealth would lead to an increase in expected profits and to a decline in borrowing. On the other hand, for the marginal firm expected profits would decline and hence the marginal firm would reject the project and put its wealth in a safe asset. Lensink and Sterken (2001) show that a reinterpretation of the Stiglitz-Weiss model, by taking into account that firms who are planning to invest may have an option to wait, will also lead to results in line with the De Meza and Webb model.

4. Credit rationing becomes irrelevant if there are many groups of borrowers

Riley (1987) changes the main focus of the Stiglitz-Weiss model by shifting attention to the total demand for bank funds. While Stiglitz and Weiss address the demand for credit primarily by considering a pool of observationally identical loan applicants, Riley examines the effects of interest rate changes across different risk pools. He shows that credit rationing of type 2 probably becomes empirically unimportant when many groups of loan applicants exist. Riley starts by showing that the assumption of a fully competitive banking industry implies that banks do not make profits and hence that the lending rate will become equal to an exogenously given interest rate on loanable funds that banks have to pay. In this setting, Riley derives a demand function for loanable funds by banks. Moreover, Riley assumes that there are many pools of observationally identical borrowers. For each group of borrowers there is a lending rate that gives the maximum expected return for banks. Until the interest rate reaches its optimal level, the derived demand function for banks is continuously decreasing in the interest rate on loanable funds. Beyond the optimal level the derived demand drops to zero. Hence, the derived demand curve has a discontinuity at the interest rate which gives the optimal return for banks. For each risk class such a derived demand curve can be drawn and for each risk class a discontinuity exists at (a different) optimal rate. By aggregating the derived demand curves of all observationally equal pools of loan applicants, the aggregate derived demand curve for loanable funds by banks can be obtained. The maximum return for banks increases with the expected return of firms, which implies that loan applicants of a pool with an expected higher mean return have a discontinuity at a higher bank borrowing rate. In this setting, all pools of loan applicants associated with an optimal lending rate below the equilibrium costs of borrowing will be excluded from lending activity (*type 1 credit rationing* or *redlining*). In other words, the groups of borrowers with a discontinuity in the derived demand curve below the cost of funds for banks are not able to borrow anything. On the other hand, for all pools of loan applicants with an optimal lending rate above the cost of borrowing supply will equal demand, and neither type 1 nor type 2 credit rationing occurs. Only for the pool of loan applicants for which the optimal lending rate equals the equilibrium cost of borrowing does type 2 credit rationing exist. If there are many groups of observationally identical borrowers, it follows that the type of credit rationing on which Stiglitz and Weiss focus will not be empirically relevant. Stiglitz and Weiss (1987) respond to this criticism by stating that their 1981 paper was meant to show which kind of imperfections could arise in the case of asymmetric information. The construction of the model was, deliberately, as simple as possible. Using these simple assumptions, the problem Riley points out could arise. However, as is shown in Stiglitz and Weiss (1983), in a somewhat more complicated setting, for instance by allowing banks and borrowers to develop multiperiod relationships, asymmetric information may lead to rationing of several or all identical pools of loan applicants. To conclude this section it is relevant to emphasize once more the importance of the Stiglitz-Weiss model. The model may be criticized on many points. Nevertheless, it can still be seen as a very important contribution to the understanding of the effects of asymmetric information for the credit market.

2.3.2 The Myers-Majluf Model

Myers and Majluf (1984) apply the Stiglitz-Weiss ideas to the problem of equity finance. Their model is a signalling model that readdresses the so-called *pecking order* or *finance hierarchy* theories (see also Myers, 1982). The firm's managers are assumed to have full information about the value of the firm's existing assets and the returns from new investment projects. If internal funds are large enough the neoclassical model applies. But if a firm exhausts its internal funds and is required to finance new projects by issuing equity, information problems might arise. There are *old* and *new* shareholders. Old shareholders are those who hold shares at the time the decision is made. The manager acts in the interest of old shareholders. External suppliers of funds cannot distinguish the quality of the firms. So the occurrence of lemons makes new shareholders ask for a premium to purchase the shares of relatively good firms to offset the losses that will arise from funding the lemons. The premium can raise the cost of new equity finance faced by managers of relatively high-quality firms above the opportunity cost of internal finance faced by existing shareholders. The underpricing of equity, due to asymmetric information, may be so severe that a firm rejects its project even if its net present value is positive. This may lead to an underinvestment problem.

The underinvestment problem can be avoided if the firms can finance their new projects by internal funds or low risk debt. The reason is that these types of finance are not underpriced by the market and hence are preferred to equity by firms. This is the *pecking order* theory of financing: firms then finance new investment internally, then with low risk debt, and finally with equity.

Myers and Majluf show that new shares will only be issued if:

$$\frac{R^*}{I} \geq \frac{R}{V} \qquad (2.15)$$

where R^* denotes the return from a new project for a good firm, R the true gross returns from assets in place for a good firm, I the cost of the new investment, and V the market value assigned to both the good firms and the lemons. This condition is equal to the requirement that the marginal q on the new project is at least equal to the ratio of the firm's true average q to the average q assigned to all firms by the market. With perfect information this ratio is equal to unity. With imperfect information this ratio will increase for good firms.

A more precise description of the Myers-Majluf model runs as follows. *Financial slack S* is defined as the sum of cash on hand and marketable securities. It represents liquid assets. Financial slack also includes the amount of default-risk-free debt. Investment I can be financed by issuing stock E or drawing from financial slack: $I = E + S$. The firm is assumed to have one existing asset (A) and one opportunity to invest. The investment opportunity loses value if not taken at time $t = 0$ and is an *all or nothing* decision. It is assumed that with respect to publicly available information capital markets are perfect and efficient. There are no transaction costs in issuing stock. The only uncertainty important for the problem stems from managers special information. Managers have special information about the firm but not about the market or the economy.

There are three periods in the model:

1. $t = -1$. The market has the same information as the manager. The expected value of the firm's asset in place is $\bar{A} = E[\hat{A}]$, where $\hat{A}$ represents the possible updates of the asset value. The NPV of the investment opportunity is $\bar{B} = E[\hat{B}]$. Slack S is known to managers and investors, as is

the distribution of $\hat{A}$ and $\hat{B}$.

2. $t = 0$. Management receives additional information about the firm's assets in place and the investment opportunity and updates their values accordingly. a is the updated value of $\hat{A}$, b is the updated value of $\hat{B}$. Negative values for both are ruled out. Management acts in the interest of old shareholders, the ones who own shares at time $t = 0$. Let V^{old} be the *intrinsic* value of the old shares. P' is the *market value* of the old shares at $t = 0$ if stock is issued and P if not. Old shareholders are assumed to sit tight. They simply do not adjust their portfolios.

3. $t = 1$. The market receives the extra information about a, b, S. Symmetric information rules again.

First, we discuss a model without debt issuing. It is assumed that $0 \le S \le I$, so the project needs to be financed with by issuing stock: $E = I - S$. Suppose the firm does not invest. In that case the intrinsic value of the old stock is equal to:

$$V^{old} = S + a \qquad (2.16)$$

the financial slack plus the realized value of the asset-in-place. If the firm does invest, the intrinsic total value of the firm will be equal to the sum of slack S, assets in place a, the investment opportunity b plus the new shares E: $S + E + a + b$. Its market value will be equal to the value of the old stock P' plus the share issuing E: $P' + E$. So the intrinsic value of the old stock will be:

$$V^{old} = \frac{P'}{P' + E}(S + E + a + b) \qquad (2.17)$$

and of the new stock:

$$V^{new} = \frac{E}{P' + E}(S + E + a + b) \qquad (2.18)$$

Old stockholders are better off if:

$$\frac{E}{P' + E}(S + a) \le \frac{P'}{P' + E}(E + b) \qquad (2.19)$$

The share of existing slack and assets going to new stockholders is less than or equal to the share of the increment to firm value obtained by old stockholders. It all depends on the joint distribution of $\hat{A}$ and $\hat{B}$ whether the firm will invest and issue equity. For low values of b and high values of a the firm will not invest even if there is a positive NPV.

The problem with this model is that the market value of old shares P'

depends on $\hat{A}$ and $\hat{B}$. If M' denotes the region of $\hat{A}$ and $\hat{B}$ where the firm invests and M for the region where the firm does not invest, the stock issue will be fairly priced for investors if:

$$P' = S + E[\hat{A}|E = I - S] + E[\hat{B}|E = I - S] = S + \bar{A}(M') + \bar{B}(M') \qquad (2.20)$$

So slack has value, because without it the firm is sometimes unwilling to issue stock and therefore misses a good investment opportunity. It is important to see what the model says about the effect of stock issues on the price of stock. If the firm is sure to issue the new issue conveys no new information to the market and the market value of old stock has to equal the market value of old stock in case of non-investing $P' = P$. But what if the probability of issuing is less than unity? Myers and Majluf show that in that case the market value of old stock is less than in the case of non-investing: $P' < P$. $P = \bar{A}(M) + S$, the expected value of assets-in-place and slack conditional on not issuing. The investment rule shows that the reason for the firm not to invest is: $a > P'(1 + b/E) - S$. Because $b/E \geq 0$, so $a + S > P'$. Therefore P must exceed P'.

Next, Myers and Majluf adjust their model for debt financing. If the firm can issue default-risk-free debt the firm will always invest and never rejects a positive NPV project. If the firm can issue risk-bearing debt, it is shown that the average opportunity loss is less with debt than with equity. The model needs to be changed a bit. Investment can be financed by $I = S + E + D$ where D is debt. Suppose equity is issued. The intrinsic value of old stock is then equal to:

$$V^{old} = a + b + I - E_1 \qquad (2.21)$$

where E_1 is the market value of the newly issued shares at time $t = 1$, when investors learn about a and b. The issue price of shares at $t = 0$ is $E = I - S$. If $\Delta E = E_1 - E$, the new shareholders capital gain, then $V^{old} = S + a + b - \Delta E$. So the firm will only invest if $b \geq \Delta E$, *i.e.* the expected NPV must exceed the capital gain on newly issued shares. With debt, a similar condition holds: $b \geq D$. With default-risk-free debt the gain is zero, so all positive NPV projects are undertaken. Issuing equity signals that additional profits will be $b - \Delta E$, while issuing debt signals profits $b - \Delta D$, therefore equity issuing signals $\Delta E < \Delta D$. But option theory shows that the value of ΔE will always exceed the value of ΔD. So only when $\Delta E < 0$, would equity financing be likely, but this implies a loss for new share holders. Therefore debt financing is more likely.

A number of papers oppose the *pecking order* hypothesis put forward by Myers and Majluf. The most prominent ones are by Brennan and Kraus (1987), Noe (1988), and Constantinides and Grundy (1989). The main idea is that firms have more financial possibilities than in the original model. As a result this does not lead directly to underinvestment.

2.3.3 Agency Theory

Agency theory is used in many types of economic problems, such as the share-cropping models in development economics and the financial models relevant for this chapter. The starting point of agency theory is the difference in objectives for a principal, the economically powerful entity, and an agent. Agency theory assumes that the principal tries to devise contractual arrangements with one or more agents in such a way that it best serves the objectives of the principal. In a general setting the problem comes down to choosing a contractual arrangement between the principal and the agent which maximizes the objective function for the principal, subject to so-called incentive and participation constraints. The agent, given the terms of the contract, behaves optimally. Normally it is assumed that the principal knows the optimal level of action of the agent for each possible contract. Therefore, the principal is able to devise the contract in such a way that the action is optimal for the principal. This is the incentive constraint. However, since the agent may be able to refuse the contract, in general the principal should also take a participation constraint into account in the construction of the optimal contract. This implies that the utility the agent earns if he accepts the contract should at least be equal to the utility he would earn when the contract is not accepted, the so-called reservation utility.

Any model in which managers have objectives different from those of shareholders is an agency model. The *principle* in these models is the shareholder and the *agent* is the manager. A clear overview of agency theory in relation to the capital structure theory is given by Hart (1995). The references in this line of literature are Fama and Miller (1972) and Jensen and Meckling (1976). Jensen (1986) presents an informal analysis. For reasons of space we give a brief discussion (see Harris and Raviv, 1991, for an extended survey).

Agency theory emphasizes conflicts between insiders vis-à-vis the firm (management) and outsiders (security-holders) and between debt and equity holders. These conflicts may result in a wedge between the cost of internal and external finance. The first type of conflict originates from the fact that the manager bears the entire cost of activities, but not the full 100 per cent gain, because managers hold less than 100 per cent of the residual claim. As a result, managers might invest in non-value maximizing activities (expensive cars, for instance). In this type of models, debt finance is considered a necessary mechanism to mitigate conflicts between equity holders and management. There are several reasons for this. First, debt financing reduces the amount of *free cash* available for managers, and thereby reduces the problem (Jensen, 1986). Second, in the case where managers want to continue firms' operation, even when a firm's cash flow is poor, debt can be a tool by which the liquidation of the firm is forced (Harris and Raviv, 1990, 1991). Related to this, debt may reduce a manager's tendency towards empire building, which may even lead them to carry out negative NPV projects (Stulz, 1990).

The second type of conflict arises from the fact that an investment project yields large returns equity holders will capture most of the gain, while in the case of loss debt holders bear the consequences. In a highly leveraged firm the incentives for shareholders to push managers to pursue riskier projects can result in an asset substitution problem. This incentive of leveraged equity holders to choose risky, negative NPV projects can be reduced by reputation. Reputation may be the reason firms opt for safer projects.

Diamond (1989) stresses that firm reputation leads to lower borrowing costs. Older, more established firms find it ideal to invest in safe projects, while younger firms opt for the riskier projects. This suggests that younger firms have less leverage. Hirshleifer and Thakor (1989) discuss the managers' reputation. Managers maximize the probability of a project success while shareholders prefer expected return. This behaviour of managers reduces the agency costs of debt. Thus firms with reputation-sensitive managers will have higher leverage.

2.4 THE IMPORTANCE OF INTERNAL FUNDS

In a neoclassical world, there is no wedge between internal and external costs of funds. However, a wedge between internal and external costs of funds can occur due to the existence of hidden information (in the Stiglitz-Weiss models, as well as the Myers-Majluf model) and agency costs. Kaplan and Zingales (1997) remark that a wedge between internal and external costs of funds can be seen as the broadest explanation for the existence of financial constraints. An increase in the wedge means that the firm becomes more financially constrained. An important question is how a wedge between costs of internal and external funds, *i.e.* the existence of capital market imperfections, affects corporate investment. In order to explain the effects of capital market imperfections on investment, it is relevant to consider the paper by Kaplan and Zingales (1997).

Kaplan and Zingales (1997) consider a firm that chooses the level of investment to maximize profits in a simple one-period model. The return to investment is $F(I)$ with $F'() > 0$ and $F'' < 0$. Investment can be financed with internal funds W or external funds E. The opportunity cost of internal funds is the cost of capital R, which is assumed to be equal to 1. The additional cost of external funds is given by a function $C(E, k)$, where k is a measure of a firm's wedge between the internal and external cost of funds. Because of information or agency problems the use of external funds generates a deadweight cost, which is borne by the issuing firm. The total cost of raising external funds increases with the amount of funds raised and in the extent of the agency or information problems: $C_E > 0$ and $C_k > 0$. Therefore the firm maximizes:

$$\Pi = F(I) - C(I - W, k) - I \tag{2.22}$$

where we substituted the restriction $I = W + E$. It is assumed that the cost function is convex in E. The first-order condition then reads:

$$F_1(I) = 1 + C_1(I - W, k) \tag{2.23}$$

Total differentiation of this condition gives:

$$F_{11}dI = C_{11}dI - C_{11}dW + C_{12}dk \tag{2.24}$$

Now we can express the sensitivity of investment to internal wealth, for given k:

$$\frac{dI}{dW} = \frac{C_{11}}{C_{11} - F_{11}} \tag{2.25}$$

In the case of perfect capital markets $dI/dW = 0$, because $C(.) = 0$. But with imperfect capital markets, this is not the case. When $C_{11} > 0$ (C is convex), and $F_{11} < 0$ (a concave technology function) the existence of capital market imperfections makes investment sensitive to internal funds. The effect of an increase in the wedge on investment, for a given W, can now also be derived. It equals:

$$\frac{dI}{dk} = \frac{-C_{12}}{C_{11} - F_{11}} \tag{2.26}$$

This is always negative if $C_{12} > 0$. In other words, if the marginal cost of raising external finance is increasing in k, an increase in capital market imperfections negatively affects investment.

2.5 CONCLUSIONS

This chapter reviews the literature on capital market imperfections and corporate investment. A distinction is made between neoclassical explanations of corporate investment and theories based on market imperfections. Capital market imperfections imply that internal and external costs of funds differ. If this is the case, the financial structure becomes an important determinant of corporate investment. More precisely, if firms are faced with capital market imperfections, corporate investment becomes sensitive to internal funds. The next question is what empirical studies say about the presence and importance of financing constraints for corporate investment.This will be the focus point of the next chapter.

NOTES

1. Grossman and Hart (1979) address this problem and advocate the *competitive price perceptions* approach. They assume that each investor bases his estimate of the market value of an investment project on the value obtained by using his own present-value vector. The problem is that some of the dividend may not lie in the marketed subspace. Forming expectations in this way does not assume that the investor has more knowledge than embedded in the equilibrium prices. Under this method the problem of finding an objective function for the corporation which aggregates the divergent opinions of the shareholders is equivalent to the problem of finding an objective function for partnership. Consumers maximize utility, and producers choose the optimal technology. Prices clear markets, and there is no government interference.

3. Investment and Capital Market Imperfections: Empirics

3.1 INTRODUCTION

The previous chapter explained the most important theoretical contributions in the field of investment and capital market imperfections. This chapter deals with empirical studies regarding this issue. Already decades ago different scholars tried to examine the relationship between financial variables and investment; see, for instance, Tinbergen (1939), Butters and Lintner (1945), Meyer and Kuh (1957), Duessenberry (1958) and Meyer and Glauber (1964). The revival of neoclassical insights in the 1960s hindered this progress; notable exceptions are Eisner (1978) and Clark (1979). More recently, many studies again try to empirically assess the effect of capital markets on investment behaviour. Basically three types of models are applied: [1]

- the reduced form accelerator type or q investment model;
- the structural investment model approach, based on the standard neoclassical Euler equation, and
- VAR models.

The next three sections describe in detail these three types of empirical investment models. Section 3.5 gives a summary of this chapter.

First, however, some evidence on the importance of internal funds in financing investment is presented in Table 3.1. Corbett and Jenkinson (1997), in a comparative study of Germany, Japan, the UK and the US present these results. The figures for internal finance are remarkably high. Bank financing and bond financing are second in line. New equity is even negative in some countries due to takeovers. Other estimates can be found in Rajan and Zingales (1996), Wald (1995), and Moret, Ernst and Young (1996) for the Netherlands. The importance of internal funds strongly suggests that firms are faced with capital market imperfections. The share of internal finance is so high that it even suggests that all firms are faced with financing constraints in one way or another. This subject will be discussed in more detail in the following sections.

Table 3.1   Net sources of finance: 1970-94

	Germany	Japan	UK	US
FINANCIAL STRUCTURE				
Internal	78.9	69.9	93.3	96.1
Bank Finance	11.9	26.7	14.6	11.1
Bonds	−1.0	4.0	4.2	15.4
New equity	0.1	3.5	− 4.6	−7.6
Trade credit	−1.2	−5.0	−0.9	−2.4
Capital transfers	8.7	.	1.7	.
Other	1.4	1.0	0.0	−4.4
Statistical adjustment	1.2	0.0	−8.4	−8.3

All percentages. *Source*: Corbett and Jenkinson (1997, p.74). The estimates are flow estimates.

3.2   REDUCED FORM INVESTMENT MODELS

Most empirical research on capital market imperfections and corporate investment is based on reduced form investment models. In the literature three different specifications of the reduced form investment models have been applied: an accelerator type investment model, a q model of investment, and a combination of these models.[2] The accelerator type model is fairly standard in the investment literature. The basic determinant of investment behaviour is the change in total sales (ΔSAL). A positive relationship between investment and the sales variable is expected if it is assumed that investment decisions are based on observed patterns of past demand for final output. The q theory of investment states that all fluctuations in investment are related to q, *i.e.* the ratio of the market value of installed capital to the replacement cost of installed capital. An increase in q should have a positive effect on investment (I). In most empirical q models, q is a catch-all proxy variable representing expectations with respect to profitability.

In order to examine effects of capital market imperfections, variables that may say something about financial constraints are added to the basic reduced form equation of investment. Based on the idea that investments are only sensitive to internal funds if there are financial constraints (see Chapter 2), it is common to include a measure of internal sources. The standard measure used in the empirical literature is cash flow (CF), measured as net profits after taxes plus depreciation. However, since most firms are likely to be financially constrained in some sense, the investment-cash flow sensitivity would be positive for almost all firms. Therefore, following Fazzari *et al.* (1988a), it is common to divide firms into groups for which it may be expected *ex ante* that differences exist with respect to the extent of financial constraints. The investment-cash flow sensitivity of the different subsamples is then compared in order to test whether different types of firms are indeed faced more with financial constraints than others. A greater cash flow sensitivity of investment is seen as an indication that the firm faces more severe capital market constraints.

The investment equation estimated in the accelerator type of models is as follows:

$$\left(\frac{I}{K}\right)_{it} = a_i + b\left(\frac{\Delta SAL}{K}\right)_{it} + c\left(\frac{CF}{K}\right)_{it} + \varepsilon_{it} \qquad (3.1)$$

To avoid heteroskedasticity, the variables are usually scaled by the capital stock (K). If capital market imperfections are absent, parameter c should be zero. Moreover, the firms that are more financially constrained should have a higher value for c.

Standard criticism of the above relationship points out that the measures of internal funds may also proxy for the profitability of investment. According to this criticism, one should expect a positive relationship between internal sources and investment, since firms with more liquidity are doing well and therefore have better possibilities to invest (Hoshi *et al.*, 1991, p.43). This may pose problems when one wants to interpret the cash flow coefficients in terms of representing capital market imperfections. Due to this criticism, the Tobin's q model is used very often. The model then looks like this: [3]

$$\left(\frac{I}{K}\right)_{it} = a_i + bq_{it} + c\left(\frac{CF}{K}\right)_{it} + \varepsilon_{it} \qquad (3.2)$$

Note that in some models the change in sales as well as in q are included simultaneously.

Fazzari *et al.* (1988a) are the first to estimate such a q model. They use an *a priori* classification of firms according to the dividend payout ratio. Low dividend payout indicates a large investment-cash flow sensitivity (and so a large c). Using a panel of 421 firms they found significant estimates of c, even when additional controls for investment opportunities were introduced (such as user cost of capital or sales).

Since the publication of the study by Fazzari *et al.* (1988a) a huge amount of similar studies appeared. In general, these studies have provided evidence of the importance of financial constraints for firms' investment decisions in the sense that the coefficient of the cash flow variable is found to be higher for firms that are supposed to be faced with severe financial constraints. For reasons of space, it is impossible to give a detailed description of these studies. The analysis will be restricted to an enumeration of reduced form investment studies published recently. This will be done in two tables: Table 3.2 presents studies for countries other than the US, and Table 3.3 presents studies which deal with the US only.

Table 3.2   Reduced form investment models applied to non-US countries

Study	Country
Deloof (1996)	Belgium
Schaller (1993)	Canada
Chirinko and Schaller (1995)	Canada
Jaramillo *et al.* (1996)	Ecuador
Elston (1996)	Germany
Frisse *et al.* (1993)	Germany
Audretsch and Elston (1994)	Germany
Elston and Albach (1994)	Germany
Fohlin (1998)	Germany
Siregar (1995)	Indonesia
Harris *et al.* (1994)	Indonesia
Rondi *et al.* (1994)	Italy
Galeotti *et al.* (1994)	Italy
Hoshi *et al.* (1991)	Japan
Van Ees and Garretsen (1994)	Netherlands
Alonso-Borrego and Bentolila (1994)	Spain
Devereux and Schiantarelli (1990)	UK
Blundell *et al.* (1992)	UK
Chapman *et al.* (1994)	UK
Scaramozzino (1997)	UK
Guariglia (1997)	UK
Bond *et al.* (1994)	Belgium, France, Germany, UK
Chirinko (1996)	Canada, Germany, Japan, Uk, US
Atiyas (1992)	Korea
Kadapakkam *et al.* (1998)	US, UK, Canada, France, Germany, Japan
Hermes and Lensink (1998a, 1998b)	Chili

A number of issues require attention:

1.   The *a priori* classification of firms in different groups;

2.   The use of the investment-cash flow sensitivity as a measure of financial constraints, and

3.   The problems related to the measurement of q.[4]

3.2.1   The *A Priori* Classification of Firms

As mentioned earlier, it is common to divide firms into subsamples based on criteria which identify *ex ante* the firms that face the most severe financial

Table 3.3   Reduced form investment models applied to the US

Fazzari *et al.* (1988a, 1988b, 1993)
Himmelberg (1991)
Hall (1991)
Oliner and Rudebusch (1992)
Himmelberg and Petersen (1994)
Petersen and Rajan (1994)
Gross (1994)
Zakrajcek (1994, 1995)
Vogt (1994)
Blanchard *et al.* (1994)
Kashyap and Stein (1994)
Calem and Rizzo (1994)
Gilchrist and Himmelberg (1995)
Berger and Udell (1995)
Calomiris and Hubbard (1995)
Gilchrist and Zakrajcek (1995a, 1995b)
Schiantarelli and Sembenelli (1995)
Carpenter *et al.* (1994)
Hsiao and Tahmiscioglu (1996)
Kaplan and Zingales (1997)
Lamont (1997)
Hansen (1999)

constraints. In the literature different criteria have been used to distinguish groups of firms. We have already mentioned the dividend payout ratio. [5] Many other criteria are used; the most important are: the age of firms, the size of firms, and whether or not a firm belongs to a business conglomerate. [6]

Concerning the age criterion, it is assumed that younger firms are confronted with capital market constraints more than older firms. The reason is that older firms are better able to communicate information with private banks since banks have had more time to obtain information on their creditworthiness. Chirinko and Schaller (1995, p.529) state that older firms have proved to be creditworthy and are willing to pay back their obligations from the past. Examples of studies in which the age criterion is used are: Devereux and Schiantarelli (1990), Oliner and Rudebusch (1992), Jaramillo *et al.* (1996), and Hermes and Lensink (1998b).

With respect to the size criterion it is generally assumed that larger firms are faced with less capital market imperfections than smaller firms since banks have fewer problems in screening and monitoring them. The reason is that information gathering has the characteristics of a fixed cost, and hence, since the volume of lending to large firms is in general quite high, the monitoring and screening costs are relatively low per unit of capital. However, some authors state that the size criterion is ambiguous since smaller firms often have more concentrated ownership and managers hold a substantial part of the common stock, so that agency problems can be overcome (see Hu and Schiantarelli, 1998). If this is the case, larger firms would be faced with more severe capital market constraints. The size criterion is used in all studies incorporating the above mentioned age criterion. In addition, size is also used in Gertler and Gilchrist (1994), and Harris *et al.* (1994).

Finally, firms that belong to a business conglomerate are assumed to have fewer problems in obtaining external funds. This is explained by the fact that very often close relationships exist between firms and banks within these conglomerates. Well known examples are the universal banking model in Germany (see Fohlin, 1998), the *Keiretsu* structure in Japan, the *coordination centre* structure in Belgium or the *Gruppo's* in Chile. Hoshi *et al.* (1991) provide evidence for the importance of conglomerates in explaining differences in investment finance between related and nonrelated firms in the case of Japan. Van Ees and Garretsen (1994) analyse the importance of informal networks within conglomerates to explain differences in firms' access to capital markets in the Netherlands. Harris *et al.* (1994) and Siregar (1995) provide evidence for the importance of conglomerates in Indonesia. Finally, Hermes and Lensink (1998a) show that related firms in Chili (so-called Gruppo's) were less restricted in attracting debt finance than nongroup related firms.

Due to the above ideas, some studies use the reduced form investment approach to test whether internal capital markets of diversified firms are efficient. A recent example is Shin and Stulz (1998). They estimate a standard accelerator type of investment model for different segments of a single firm. In the investment equations both the cash flow for the segment under consideration and the sum of the cash flow of the other segments are included. This has been done for firms with limited diversification and for highly diversified firms. Shin and Stultz find, both for the diversified and for limited diversified firms, that the sensitivity of a segments investment to its own cash flow is much higher than to the cash flow of other segments. They also find that the sensitivity of a segment's investment to other segments, cash flow does not depend on its investment opportunities. These results indicate that the internal capital market plays a limited role and that the internal capital market is not efficient. [7]

After this short digression concerning the efficiency of internal capital markets, we return to the discussion concerning the *a priori* classification of firms. Although a huge amount of studies have used this approach and still do, the division of firms in groups according to an *a priori* time invariant financing constraint is not undisputed. Hu and Schiantarelli (1998) mention the following drawbacks. First, it may be the case that a multiplicity of factors determine whether a firm is confronted with financial constraints. This cannot be picked up with the single indicator approach normally used. Second, during the sample period it may be the case that a firm that is initially faced with severe financial constraints becomes less financially constrained later. This will especially be the case when the extent of capital market imperfections depends on the general macroeconomic environment. Hence, although it is possible to identify possibly constrained firms, it is quite often impossible to identify the years during which a firm is constrained. This makes it almost impossible to differentiate between firm-specific effects on investment and the effects of financing constraints (Kaplan and Zingales, 1997). Finally, the variable used to select firms is probably correlated with the endogenous variable investment. In that case, the analysis suffers from selection bias.

There are several ways around these problems. One possibility would be to allow the indicator for the availability of internal funds to interact with a time-varying variable proxing relevant firm characteristics, instead of selecting firms on the basis of *ex ante* time-invariant indicators. This would tackle the problem that firms may move from one regime to another during the sample period. If the size-criterion is used as the relevant firm characteristic, the equation to be estimated is:

$$\left(\frac{I}{K}\right)_{it} = a_i + bq_{it} + c\left(\frac{CF}{K}\right)_{it} + d\left(\frac{CF}{K}\right) * SIZE + \varepsilon_{it} \qquad (3.3)$$

This equation is estimated for all firms in the sample. By differentiating Equation (3.3) the effect of the size of the firm on the cash flow coefficient becomes clear:

$$\frac{d(I/K)}{d(CF/K)} = c + d * SIZE \qquad (3.4)$$

Since larger firms are assumed to have fewer problems in communicating information with banks and therefore are probably less financially constrained, the sign of d is expected to be negative. This approach is often used in the investment literature, see for instance Ghosal (1991), who used *SIZE* as an interaction term to account for differences in demand uncertainty influenced by the size of the firm. The interaction approach also allows the instrumental variable technique to be used by which the endogeneity problem could be overcome. The interaction approach, by taking into account several interaction terms, may also give rise to the problem related to the existence of several important factors. However, if the range of important factors is large, this becomes difficult.

Another possibility, recently suggested and applied in the paper by Hu and Schiantarelli (1998), is to use an endogenous switching model. Based on an earlier paper of Dickens and Lang (1985), Hu and Schiantarelli endogenously determine the premium on external finance (in other words the wedge) by a switching function. The switching function depends on a range of variables that are suggested to be important indicators for the extent to which firms are confronted with financial constraints. Hu and Schiantarelli, in their basic version of the model, use different financial variables, a measure of size, and year and industry dummies in their switching function. In a more general specification they also include q in the switching function. The switching function determines whether a firm can be classified as a high or a low premium firm, *i.e.* a firm confronted with more or less severe capital market imperfections.

Their model is based on the framework of the q investment model, and, if we ignore the industry and year dummies, is formulated as follows:

$$\left(\frac{I}{K}\right)_{it} = \beta_1^{lp} q_{it} + \beta_2^{lp} \left(\frac{CF}{K}\right)_{it} + \varepsilon_{it} \tag{3.5}$$

if

$$Z_{it}\gamma + \mu_{it} < 0 \tag{3.6}$$

and

$$\left(\frac{I}{K}\right)_{it} = \beta_1^{hp} q_{it} + \beta_2^{hp} \left(\frac{CF}{K}\right)_{it} + \varepsilon_{it} \tag{3.7}$$

if

$$Z_{it}\gamma + \mu_{it} \geq 0 \tag{3.8}$$

where Z is the vector of variables in the switching function, ε and μ are error terms and hp and lp denote high and low-premium, respectively. By maximizing a log-likelihood function, Hu and Schiantarelli (1998) are able to jointly estimate the parameters $\beta_1^{hp}, \beta_2^{hp}, \beta_1^{lp}, \beta_2^{lp}$ and γ. The model is applied to a panel of US manufacturing firms. The results can be used to determine the probability that a firm will operate in the low or high premium regime. Moreover, they can show whether an increase in the different factors in the switching function implies a higher or a lower probability of being in the high premium regime. It appears that an increase in financial weakness variables, an increase in size, and a decrease in q leads to an increase in the probability of being in the high premium regime. The relationship between q and the probability of being in one or another regime is explained by assuming that firms with a high q have fewer agency problems. Finally, it appears that the probability of being in a high premium regime depends on macroeconomic conditions.

Fazzari *et al.* distinguish three classes of firms that face financing decisions depending on the dividend to income ratio. Hansen (1999) notes two problems in this approach. First, the dividend payout ratio is assumed to be exogenous, while theory treats the dividend decision as endogenous. Secondly, the threshold values are set arbitrarily. Hansen proposes to use the ratio of cash flow to total assets as a threshold variable to classify firms into subgroups and to estimate threshold value. His results support the finding of two thresholds as in the original Fazzari *et al.* paper.

3.2.2 The Investment-Cash Flow Sensitivity as a Measure of Financial Constraints

Some authors strongly oppose the use of the investment-cash flow sensitivity as a measure of financial constraints. The most prominent critics of this approach are Kaplan and Zingales (1997). It is useful to survey their argument by using the model, as presented in the previous section. Kaplan and Zingales remark that the usual practice of comparing the investment-cash flow sensitivities across groups of firms corresponds to looking at differences in dI/dW as a function of internal wealth W or the wedge between the costs of external and internal capital k. This approach is only useful if the sensitivity of investment to cash flow (dI/dW) decreases when a firm's availability of internal liquidity increases. In other words, d^2I/dW^2 should be negative.

In order to calculate the second derivative, we make use of the result that if $H(W,I) = 0$ and $I = f(W)$ is a solution, $f''(W)$ is given by:

$$f'' = -\frac{H_{11}''(H_2')^2 - 2H_{12}''H_1'H_2' + H_{22}''(H_1')^2}{(H_2')^3} \quad (3.9)$$

In our case, we use a profit function specified as $\Pi = F(I) - C(W - I, k) - I$. Differentiating this profit function with respect to I gives $F_1(I) - C_1(I - W, k) - 1 = 0$. This corresponds to $H(W,I) = 0$ in the above example. H_1' by definition is the first derivative of H with respect to W. In our case this equals C_{11}. Similarly, the first derivative of H with respect to I (H_2') equals $F_{11} - C_{11}$. This implies that:

$$
\begin{aligned}
H_{11}'' &= -C_{111} \\
H_{12}'' &= C_{111} \\
H_{22}'' &= F_{111} - C_{111}
\end{aligned}
$$

It can now be derived that:

$$f'' = -\frac{-C_{111}(F_{11} - C_{11})^2 - 2C_{111}C_{11}(F_{11} - C_{11}) + (F_{111} - C_{111})C_{11}^2}{(F_{11} - C_{11})^3} \quad (3.10)$$

Therefore:

$$\frac{d^2I}{dW^2} = \frac{F_{111}C_{11}^2 - C_{111}F_{11}^2}{(C_{11} - F_{11})^3} \quad (3.11)$$

Assuming that C_{11} and F_{11} are both unequal to zero:

$$\frac{d^2I}{dW^2} = \left(\frac{F_{111}}{F_{11}^2} - \frac{C_{111}}{C_{11}^2}\right) \frac{F_{11}^2 C_{11}^2}{(C_{11} - F_{11})^3} \qquad (3.12)$$

The second term is always positive. d^2I/dW^2 is negative if and only if the first term is negative. This condition implies that at the optimal level of investment there should be a certain relationship between the curvature of the production function and the curvature of the cost function. Kaplan and Zingales argue that for a quadratic cost function and a production function with a negative third derivative, such as a technology function I^ρ with $0 < \rho < 1$, the investment-cash flow sensitivity increases with the firm's internal liquidity. Hence, when financial constraints become more severe, the sensitivity of investment to cash flow does not necessarily increase.

Another problem with investment-cash flow sensitivity as an indicator for financial constraints is addressed by Jensen (1986). He argues that the investment-cash flow correlation may reflect nonvalue maximizing behaviour by managers, rather than financing constraints. Jensen's argument is based on agency theory and labelled the *free cash flow* approach. Changes in net worth are linked with corporate expenditure, holding constant investment opportunities. Managers use internal funds for nonvalue maximizing activities in their own interest. This hypothesis is hard to test, although Blanchard *et al.* (1994) do it. Hubbard *et al.* (1995) show that mature low-payout firms (those emphasized by the free cash flow approach) account for the rejection of the frictionless model among low-dividend payout firms. This indirect test suggests that the free cash flow approach is not empirically supported. On the other hand, Kadapakkam *et al.* (1998), in a study of 6 OECD countries, argue that investment-cash flow sensitivity is more the result of managerial agency considerations than of capital market constraints. Their argument is based on the fact that they find higher cash flow sensitivities for large firms than for small firms, which in their view cannot be explained by capital market imperfections theory since large firms are more capital constrained than small firms. Therefore they conclude that the investment-cash flow sensitivity cannot be a good measure for financial constraints but is more related to managerial considerations. This way of reasoning, however, totally ignores the fact that in the capital market imperfections literature the size criterion is also ambiguous. As has been explained above, it may well be the case that larger firms are more capital constrained than smaller firms due to agency problems. If this is the case, their results imply that investment-cash flow sensitivity is an accurate measure of access to capital markets. Finally, Fohlin (1998) in her study on the importance of the universal banking system in Germany for the period 1903-13 concludes that investment is more sensitive for bank-networked firms than unattached firms, although bank-networked firms suffered less from financial constraints. This indirectly confirms the criticism of Kaplan and Zingales on the use of investment-cash flow sensitivity as a measure of financial constraints.

3.2.3 Measurement Problems of q

Although the q theory of investment is an appealing framework for investment studies, its empirical performance is often disappointing. One of the main reasons why the q model behaves so badly is related to measurement problems. Since the marginal q is unobservable, the average q has very often been used as a proxy.[8] However, the average q is only a perfect proxy for marginal q when markets are perfectly competitive and there is a homogeneous production technology. Hence, severe measurement problems are probably introduced. Moreover, the empirical measurement of (average) q requires data on prices and number of shares outstanding, which prevents the inclusion of private and thus smaller firms in the sample (see *e.g.* Perfect and Wiles, 1994). These problems can be avoided by using a structural model approach, by directly estimating the Euler equation. This approach is the subject of the next section.

3.3 EULER EQUATION MODELS

In intertemporal investment modelling it is natural to use the Euler approach. The idea of the Euler approach is that intertemporal optimization requires optimality along the optimal path, yielding optimality conditions for adjacent periods. In our case such an optimal condition can be derived for the unrestricted neoclassical model and for a model assuming capital constraints. Testing both models should then yield information on the existence of capital market imperfections. Like the q models, the sample can be split up into categories of firms using several criteria, which *a priori* reflect the probability that a particular type of firm suffers from debt constraints. However, as shown in the previous section, this is subject to many difficulties.

The Euler approach has advantages and disadvantages. First, the advantages will be listed:

1. the approach does not need an explicit investment equation. Therefore, Tobin's q is not included and measurement problems of q can be avoided;

2. the model explicitly takes into account dynamics. Since investment models are dynamic models, this is an appealing property;

3. the model is a structural model, in which the so-called deep structural

parameters are estimated directly. This avoids all the problems related
with reduced form models.

There are also serious disadvantages:

1. Euler models do not estimate the firm's decision rule. The results are
   therefore difficult to compare with reduced form estimates;

2. Euler equation estimates are sensitive to specification and tend to have
   poor small-sample properties;

3. Euler models cannot indicate whether investors face a permanent constraint, because they only estimate the period-to-period changes in behaviour;

4. Euler equation models need to make assumptions regarding technology
   and adjustment costs just like in the literature on the q model. Therefore
   there is no real advantage here;

5. the parameterization of the so-called slack variables (see below) is not
   grounded in theory. The Lucas critique applies to the specification of
   these slacks.

Despite these disadvantages, the approach is elegant and needs to be addressed
here. The major examples are the models due to Whited (1992) and Bond
and Meghir (1994). A theoretical extension is given by Chatelain (1996) who
discusses endogenous credit ceilings. The next subsection discusses the Whited
(1992) model. The Bond and Meghir (1994) model is similar and therefore not
presented in detail.

3.3.1 The Whited Model

The Whited (1992) model is a standard in finance and elaborates on a basic
finance hierarchy model. For the sake of simplicity, it is assumed that debt
is the only source of external funds. This means that, in line with related
research, the model abstracts from the quantitatively unimportant new share
issues. Assuming that arbitrage yields equality of *ex post* and *ex ante* returns
to the firm's share holders, the (after tax) required return on investment R_{it} can
be defined as:

$$R_{it} = \frac{E_t[V_{i,t+1}] - V_{it} + E_t[d_{i,t+1}]}{V_{it}} \tag{3.13}$$

where $E_t[.]$ denotes the expectation operator, $d_{i,t+1}$ represents after tax dividends, and V_{it} is defined as the expected present value of cash flows. i and t
denote the firm and year in the panel data set. Capital gains are net of taxes.

The firm maximizes:

$$V_{i0} = E_0\left[\sum_{t=1}^{\infty} \Pi_{j=0}^{t-1}\beta_{ij}d_{it}\,|\,\Omega_0\right] \qquad (3.14)$$

where Π represents the product operator, $\beta_{ij} = 1/(1+R_{ij})$ is the firm's discount factor and Ω_0 the relevant information set at time $t = 0$. The firm's dividend is defined as:

$$d_{it} = (1-\tau)[F(K_{i,t-1},L_{it}) - w_t L_{it} - G(I_{it},K_{i,t-1}) - i_{t-1}B_{i,t-1}] +$$
$$B_{it} - (1 - \pi_t^e)B_{i,t-1} - p_{it}^I I_{it} \qquad (3.15)$$

where τ is the corporate income tax, $F(.,.)$ represents the production function, K_{it} the capital stock, L_{it} labour (or more broadly defined a vector of variable production factors), w_t the real wage rate (or the real prices of variable production factors), $G(.,.)$ a cost adjustment function, I_{it} investment, i_t the nominal interest paid on corporate debt, B_{it} the real value of net debt outstanding, π_t^e expected inflation, and p_t^I the investment price index. In each period the firm has to meet the requirement that the sum of internal resources and debt payments should be equal to production less costs. Inflation erodes debt (accounting for the inclusion of $\pi_t^e B_{1,t-1}$). Two additional conditions have to be met: first, dividends of course cannot be negative; second, the standard transversality condition of no Ponzi game must hold in order to prevent the firm from borrowing an infinite amount to pay out as dividends.

Let λ_{it} be the series of multipliers associated with the condition of nonnegative dividends. The firm decides on the capital stock K_{it} and the amount of debt B_{it}.[9] For real investment the first order condition is:

$$\beta_{it}E_t\left[\frac{1+\lambda_{i,t+1}}{1+\lambda_{it}}(F_K(K_{it},L_{i,t+1}) - G_K(I_{i,t+1},K_{it})\right.$$
$$\left.+(1-\delta)(G_I(I_{i,t+1},K_{it}) + \frac{p_{i,t+1}^I}{1-\tau}))\right] = G_I(I_{it},K_{i,t-1}) + \frac{p_{it}^I}{1-\tau} \qquad (3.16)$$

This is the neoclassical version of the Euler investment equation, which assumes absence of capital market imperfections. The right-hand side of condition (3.16) represents the marginal installation costs G_I and the current (tax adjusted) price of investing in new capital in the current period t. The left-hand side shows the costs of postponing investment until the next period $t+1$ (costs of waiting), which consists of the marginal product of the new capital foregone and the purchasing and installation costs of investing tomorrow. The opportunity cost of investing in the future is weighted by the relative shadow

value dividends (λ) in this period and the next. In equilibrium both costs are
equal. The first-order condition for borrowing reads:

$$(1 + \lambda_{it}) - \beta_{it}(1 + (1-\tau)i_t - \pi_t^e)E_t[(1 + \lambda_{i,t+1})] = 0 \qquad (3.17)$$

The discount rate of each firm must be equal to the inverse of the market interest
rate (known by the agents) in the case where internal resources are strictly
positive.

Debt constraints
In order to be able to analyse the impact of possible debt constraints, Whited
adjusts the neoclassical Euler investment equation. Suppose we have a borrow-
ing constraint, $B_{it} < B_{it}^*$ with multiplier γ_{it}. The borrowing condition (3.17) gets
an additional term:

$$(1 + \lambda_{it}) - \beta_{it}(1 + (1-\tau)i_t - \pi_t^e)E_t[(1 + \lambda_{i,t+1})] - \gamma_{it} = 0 \qquad (3.18)$$

The additional term γ_{it} introduces a wedge between the shadow value of residual earnings in the current and next period. Suppose the shadow value of dividends is higher today than it is expected to be tomorrow and the firm reaches
its debt capacity. Then, the present value of the firm can be increased with
γ by relaxing the debt constraint. The Euler approach uses two periods only.
This implies that only a change in the debt constraint between the two periods
is picked up by equation (3.18). Generally a two-period analysis will not be
sufficient to deal with the intertemporal aspects of debt constraints, however.
In reality, future expected constraints may lead to a reduction of current investment. Moreover, past debt constraints might have increased current interest
rates. So firms with former debt problems might have a higher interest burden
today.
    Substitution of (3.18) into (3.16) yields the debt-constraint augmented Euler
investment equation:

$$\frac{\beta_{it}}{1 + \gamma_{it} + E_t[\lambda_{it+1}]}E_t[(1 + \lambda_{i,t+1})(F_K(K_{it}, L_{it}) - G_K(I_{it+1}, K_{it}) +$$

$$(1-\delta)(G_I(I_{i,t+1}, K_{it}) + \frac{p_{i,t+1}^I}{1-\tau}))] = G_I(I_{it}, K_{i,t-1}) + \frac{p_{it}^I}{1-\tau} \qquad (3.19)$$

As Whited (1992, p. 1433) argues, compared to an unconstrained firm, a firm
facing a binding borrowing constraint has a higher value of γ_{it} and thus a higher
marginal opportunity cost of investing today versus delaying it until tomorrow.
To put it differently, future earnings are discounted more heavily if firms face

a binding debt constraint in the current period. If this higher discount factor is captured by the capital markets, then debt constrained firms will face higher rates of interest on debt. In other words, the borrowing constraint will lead to a firm-specific risk premium on corporate debt.

3.3.2 Empirical Examples

We will again be brief and not explain in detail all empirical results. Table 3.4 presents an overview of empirical models following the Euler approach to investment capital market imperfections relationships.

Table 3.4   *Empirical Euler equation models*

Study	Country
Gilchrist (1990)	US
Gertler *et al.* (1991)	US
Whited (1992)	US
Hubbard and Kashyap (1992)	US
Hubbard *et al.* (1995)	US
Himmelberg (1990)	US
Carpenter (1992)	US
Kwan (1994)	US
Ng and Schaller (1993)	Canada
Bond and Meghir (1994)	UK
Estrada and Vallés (1995)	Spain
Van Ees *et al.* (1998)	Netherlands
Barran and Peters (1996)	Belgium

An important distinction between the different empirical papers is worth mentioning. One line of models, following the Whited debt-constraint model, must make assumptions with respect to the parameterization of the debt constraint slack parameter. For instance, Whited uses a cubic equation in the debt-to-asset ratio and interest coverage, while Hubbard *et al.* (1995) use cash flow as a proxy. Another approach is followed by Van Ees *et al.* (1998). They do not proxy the slack parameter but use empirically observed interest rates, thereby assuming that the uniformly paid interest rate i_t in the neoclassical model needs to be replaced by a firm-specific interest rate i_{it} in the debt-constraint model. In this way, they circumvent the problem that the optimality conditions of the debt-constraint augmented model do not provide an analytical solution for the slack parameter. As Chirinko (1993, p.1903) correctly observes: "..the endogenous variables that parameterize the multiplier – such as cash flow and net worth sensitive to the firm's decisions – are not accounted for explicitly in specifying the econometric equation, thus blurring economic interpretations of the statistical tests." The parameterization of the slack parameter by means of various proxies for the financial distress of a firm is meant to take account of only that part of the difference between the unobserved i_{it} and i_t which can be attributed to the alleged existence of a premium on corporate debt. The advantage of directly measuring i_{it} is that the firm-specific interest rate necessarily includes any such premium. This conclusion is subject to one important caveat: a difference between the observed firm-specific interest rate and the neoclassical interest rate i_t need not necessarily to be the result of the existence of a premium on borrowing but might instead be a result of firm-specific factors which are unrelated to the workings of the debt market. In a similar vein one could argue that even if it is granted that the difference between i_{it} and i_t reflects the existence of a premium on corporate debt, this need not have an impact on the firm's investment behaviour as long as the firm can resort to other means of external finance, notably the issuance of new shares.

The final remark we would like to make in this section is that all models presented in Table 3.4 provide evidence for the capital market imperfections model. It appears that young and small firms that have a low dividend payout suffer most. Dividend payments are an important signalling device. In signalling models the payment of high dividends is used to separate firms with favourable inside information (see Bhattacharya, 1979).

3.4   VECTOR AUTOREGRESSION (VAR) MODELS

The problem in all cash flow type of models, estimating the importance of capital market imperfections, lies in the isolation of capital market imperfections from profitability. It is often unclear to what extent the predictive power of cash flow stems from its role as an indicator of investment opportunities or from its role in predicting capital constraints. For this reason, Tobin's q is usually included as an additional variable. Tobin's q should control for investment opportunities, so that the cash flow effect can be entirely attributed to capital constraints. However, as we have argued before, the measurement of q is quite problematic, leading to investment models with low predictive power. Therefore some authors have proposed an alternative approach in which a forecasting model is used and financial variables as proxies for marginal q are bypassed. Abel and Blanchard (1986) have proposed a shortcut and used an auxiliary econometric model to forecast future values of marginal q. A VAR is constructed to decompose the effect of cash flow on investment into two categories: one that forecasts future profitability under perfect capital markets and a residual component that may be attributable to capital market frictions.

Following Abel and Blanchard (1986), Gilchrist and Himmelberg (1995) also specify a VAR forecasting framework. They propose a so-called *fundamental q* approach, which allows them to examine to what extent the predictive power of cash flow is related to capital market imperfections on the one hand and investment opportunities (its fundamental role) on the other. They determine the expected value of marginal q – in their words fundamental q – by estimating a set of VAR forecasting equations for a subset of information available to the firm. They include fundamental q into the standard investment equation that also includes liquidity (cash flow). Since in the VAR forecasting equations cash flow is used as one of the determinants for q so that cash flows role in predicting the marginal value of capital is controlled for, all the additional predictive power of cash flow can be attributed to capital market imperfections. The model starts with:

$$\left(\frac{I}{K}\right)_{it} = \gamma_i + \frac{1}{\alpha}E[q_{it+s}|\Omega_{it}] + \varepsilon_{it} \tag{3.20}$$

where I is investment, K the capital stock, q marginal q, $E[.|\Omega_{it}]$ the expectations operator conditional on the time t information set Ω_{it}, and γ, α are coefficients. To construct a proxy for the expectations term (marginal q) the following linear AR(1) process is specified:

$$x_{it} = Ax_{it-1} + f_i + d_t + u_{it} \tag{3.21}$$

where x_{it} is a vector of firm fundamentals, f_i a firm effect, d_t a time effect and u_{it} an orthogonal innovation. By using the law of iterated expectations it can be shown that:

$$E[x_{it+s}|x_{it}] = A^s x_{it} + \Gamma_1 f_i + \Gamma_2 d_t \tag{3.22}$$

where Γ_1, Γ_2 are complicated functions of s, A, d. The next step is to introduce marginal profit as the jth element of x_{it}. Gilchrist and Himmelberg (1995) show that, under the assumption that the profit function is homogeneous of degree 1, the investment equation can be rewritten as:

$$\left(\frac{I}{K}\right)_{it} = \gamma_i + \frac{1}{\alpha}[c'(I - \lambda A)^{-1}]x_{it} + \omega_{it} + \eta_i + \nu_t + \varepsilon_{it} \tag{3.23}$$

where η_i and ν_t represent the composite firm and time effects resulting from the substitution and $\omega_{it} = \sum_{s=0}^{\infty} \lambda^s E[\pi_{it+s}|\Omega_{it}] - \sum_{s=0}^{\infty} \lambda^s P[\pi_{it+s}|x_{it}]$ is the error introduced by replacing the expected discounted value of marginal profits by its projection on x_{it}. This error is orthogonal to x_{it} by construction. c is a vector of zeros with a one in the jth row.

The estimation runs in two steps. First, the VAR is estimated. The model is estimated in first differences (not as deviations from the mean, since this is only valid if the explanatory variables are strictly exogenous) to get rid of firm-specific effects. A GMM routine is proposed using all but first order lags of x_{it}. Using the estimated values, $\hat{A}$, fundamental q is computed as $c'(I - \lambda\hat{A})^{-1}x_{it}$. In the second step the investment model is again estimated in first differences. The $\Delta\omega_{it}$ and $\Delta\varepsilon_{it}$ are orthogonal to the set of instruments in the GMM. Since F_{it} is a constructed regressor standard errors are incorrectly estimated and subsequently corrected. Finally this model is compared to a model that uses cash flow as an additional variable.

Using a sample of 428 firms for the US (*Compustat*), Gilchrist and Himmelberg (1995) find by using fundamental q more plausible estimates of adjustment costs and speeds of adjustment. Moreover they find that the *a priori* unconstrained firms satisfy the adjusted q model. Tobin's q tends to overstate the excess sensitivity of investment to cash flow particularly for unconstrained firms. Finally, it appears that for firms that are classified as financially constrained, cash flow still has predictive power, even if one controls for its role in predicting investment opportunities.

3.5   CONCLUSIONS

This chapter has reviewed the empirical literature on investment and capital market imperfections. A distinction is made between reduced form approaches to investment, the Euler approach and a VAR approach. The main problems in the empirical literature are measurement problems related to Tobin's q and how to come up with an approach that can examine to what extent corporate investment is sensitive to internal funds when a company is plagued by capital market imperfections. It seems that a lot still has to be done in this area. Finally, it is remarkable that there are almost no theoretical nor empirical studies available which try to combine the capital market imperfections and corporate investment literature, which is the subject matter of this chapter, and the corporate investment and uncertainty literature, which is the other major branch of literature attempting to provide reasonable explanations of corporate investment.

NOTES

1. In Appendix A it is shown how the q model and the Euler approach can be derived from a general model.
2. In Chapter 4 attention is also paid to the q model.
3. See Hubbard (1998) for a formal derivation of this type of model.
4. These points are also mentioned by Hubbard (1998) as the main problems of the reduced form

approach.
5. In the Euler approach firms are split in different samples as well. In such a framework, Bond and Meghir (1994) also use the dividend payout ratio.
6. Other criteria used are: information costs (for instance underwriting costs, see Calomiris and Himmelberg, 1995), leverage, interest coverage, debt-to-asset ratios, cash flow ratios, whether firms have received a bond rating at the beginning of the sample period (Whited, 1992), the degree of concentration of shareholding (Schaller, 1993), and access to public debt markets.
7. Lamont (1997) also considers the efficiency of the internal market. He studies a group of firms that have corporate segments both in the oil extraction industry and non-oil industries. He shows that investment in non-oil divisions drops significantly when the cash flow of the oil divisions decrease. This implies that corporate segments are interdependent and not treated as stand-alone firms, which suggest that internal capital markets work.
8. In convential empirical q models the beginning-of-period (BOP) average q is used. Barnett and Sakellariss (1999) show that by using BOP values of q the structural parameters of the adjustment cost function cannot be derived. They propose to use the end of period values of average q.
9. The firm also takes a labour demand decision in accordance with the marginal condition $F_L = w$.

PART TWO

Investment under Uncertainty

4. Investment under Uncertainty: Orthodox Models

4.1 INTRODUCTION

Both firm-specific and aggregate investment are central topics in economic theory. Investment plays a pivotal role in explaining the process of economic growth. Some decades ago the most important investment theories were neoclassical investment theory, e.g. the Jorgensen model, and the closely related q model of investment. These models assume that there are no capital market constraints and that the investment decision is made under certainty. Although theoretically these models are appealing, empirically they perform badly. Therefore, there have been recently many attempts to improve upon the empirical specification of investment models. These papers examine the implications of capital market imperfections and uncertainty for investment behaviour.

It is common to distinguish between fundamental or Knightian uncertainty and classical uncertainty. Unlike classical uncertainty, fundamental uncertainty assumes that uncertainty cannot be represented by probability theory, and hence probability distributions cannot be used. Classical uncertainty implies that agents are uncertain about the values of variables, but they know their probability distribution. In empirical studies only the second concept of uncertainty can be used in a meaningful way.

This chapter deals with classical uncertainty. It surveys the orthodox literature on investment under uncertainty. Chapter 5 deals with the more recent literature. Together these two chapters complement other existing surveys, that only deal with a subset of the available literature (see notably Nickell, 1978, for the orthodox studies; and Pindyck, 1991, and Dixit and Pindyck, 1994, for the newer approaches).

Many studies are available in which the relationship between investment and uncertainty is examined, making it fairly difficult to cover all relevant contributions. Therefore, the analysis is deliberately restricted to some of the most influential papers. Moreover, empirical studies on investment under uncertainty are not dealt with, and only the theoretical contributions dealing with a single firm are considered. Chapter 6 deals with empirical investment uncertainty studies. Dixit and Pindyck (1994, part IV) consider the effects of uncertainty at the industry level. Since we do not deal with these effects, we ignore issues pertaining to firm-specific (idiosyncratic) and industry-wide risk.

Orthodox investment models ignore the implications of irreversibility of and the possibility to delay the investment decision. There are two types of *orthodox* models on which we will focus. Section 4.2 considers models that ignore adjustment costs for investment. These models are static, and hence a well defined family of investment models exists. They primarily deal with the effects of uncertainty on production and the optimal input mix. Yet, the framework of these models is closely related to one of the most famous investment models: the seminal Jorgenson model. Therefore, section 4.2 starts by explaining the Jorgenson (1963) model, after which the effects of uncertainty on production and the optimal input mix are considered. Section 4.3 deals with orthodox models in which adjustment costs are taken into account. The section first explains what adjustment costs are and how they can be modelled. Next, three seminal contributions in this area are surveyed: the models by Hartman (1972), Abel (1983), and Stevens (1974) and Nickell (1978). The most important differences between these models relate to risk behaviour and the stochastic specification of uncertainty. Hartman and Abel assume that the firm is risk neutral, whereas Stevens and Nickell allow for risk averse behaviour. Concerning the stochastic specification of uncertainty, Hartman assumes that there is uncertainty in each period, including the current period. In line with most recent contributions, Abel assumes perfect certainty in the current period but uncertainty in all future periods.

4.2 ORTHODOX MODELS WITHOUT ADJUSTMENT COSTS

In the 1970s a vast number of papers on the importance of uncertainty for the behaviour of the firm were published. In many of these papers the firm's optimization problem reduces to a static optimization problem since adjustment costs with respect to labour and capital are ignored, and hence there are no intertemporal elements in the firm's maximization problem. They primarily deal with the effects of uncertainty on optimal output, and on the optimal input choice of a firm. The framework of these models can be compared to the famous neoclassical Jorgenson model, which is formulated as a dynamic model but is essentially a static model. The discussion begins with the Jorgenson model.

4.2.1 The Neoclassical Investment Model: The Jorgenson Model

The Jorgenson model is a neoclassical investment theory in which a firm produces output with capital K and labour L, using a neoclassical production function $Q(K,L)$. The neoclassical production function has positive but diminishing marginal products and satisfies the so-called Inada conditions ($Q'(0) = \infty$, $Q'(\infty) = 0$ and $Q(0) = 0$). The basis of the neoclassical model is that it allows for substitution between the two inputs. In line with regular investment theory, it is assumed that the productivity of capital is independent of its age and that it evaporates at an exponential rate.

The firm is assumed to optimize cash flow (π), written as:

$$\pi = pQ(K,L) - wL - p_k I \tag{4.1}$$

where w is the money wage rate, Q production, p the product price, p_k the price of machines, and I gross investment, defined as the sum of net investment (dK/dt) plus replacement investment (δK), where δ denotes the exponential rate of decay of the capital stock. In this specification, the firm is assumed to own its stock of capital rather than rent it from households (see below). However, households do have a claim on the firm's net cash flow.

The Jorgenson model assumes the absence of adjustment costs, perfect foresight, and that the firm is a price taker in all markets (p, w and p_k are given). The firm maximizes the present value of its net worth, which equals the sum of the discounted net future revenues to infinity:

$$V(K,L) = \int_0^\infty \left[pQ(K,L) - wL - p_k \left(\frac{dK}{dt} + \delta K \right) \right] e^{-\rho t} dt \tag{4.2}$$

where ρ is the discount rate and $e^{-\rho t}$ the discount factor. The problem is an infinite horizon problem, so that the objective functional is an improper integral. Since the discount factor is taken into account, the problem converges in the case where the term between brackets has an upper limit. The problem can be solved by using the calculus of variations (see Chiang, 1992, for a survey of dynamic optimization). One difficulty with the Jorgenson model becomes immediately clear: the integral will only converge if dK/dt is bounded. In other words, to rule out an undefined investment function dK/dt may not become infinite. Jorgenson simply does not allow K to make vertical jumps.

The method of calculus of variation uses so-called Euler conditions to find the extremes. The Euler conditions yield (see *e.g.* Chiang, 1992, p. 104):

$$F_K - \frac{d}{dt} F_{K'} = 0 \tag{4.3}$$

$$F_L - \frac{d}{dt}F_{L'} = 0 \qquad (4.4)$$

where F refers to the integrand. Applying these conditions gives: $F_K = (PQ_k - p_k\delta)e^{-\rho t}$; $F_{K'} = F_{dK/dt} = -ie^{-\rho t}$; $F_L = (pQ_L - w)e^{-\rho t}$ and $F_{L'} = 0$. Hence, for all $t \geq 0$:

$$Q_k = \frac{p_k(\rho + \delta)}{p} = \frac{c}{p} \qquad (4.5)$$

$$Q_L = \frac{w}{p} \qquad (4.6)$$

where c are the costs of capital. The first-order conditions are the standard marginality conditions, well known in the static context. Here these conditions apply to each period t. Since the right-hand sides of the above expressions are constants, this model implies a constant optimal capital stock and labour demand.

Note that the Jorgenson model is in fact not a dynamic model as its optimality conditions only include current period variables. The main reason for this result is the absence of adjustment costs, which implies that the capital stock can be adjusted costlessly at each moment in time. The first-order conditions derived from the present value maximization can be shown to be exactly the same as the first-order conditions derived from maximizing instantaneous profit (π) at each period in time. In that case, the problem is to maximize:

$$\pi = pQ(K,L) - wL - ip_kK \qquad (4.7)$$

where i equals the rental price per unit of capital services. In this formulation it is assumed that the firm hires the capital stock from households. The net return for a household that owns a unit of capital iseqaul to $i - \delta$. Under the assumption of perfect substitutability between loans and capital $i - \delta = r = \rho$, where r is the interest rate on funds lent to other households, which is assumed to be equal to the discount rate. Hence $i = \rho + \delta$. Differentiating Equation (4.7) with respect to K and L gives the same first-order conditions as the conditions of the Jorgensen model.

4.2.2   Effects of Uncertainty on Production

A drawback of ignoring adjustment costs for capital is that firms can jump immediately to the optimal capital stock.[1] This implies that the rate of investment, the rate at which capital changes over time, becomes infinite. Hence, in models without adjustment costs there is no investment function in the usual sense, and effects of uncertainty on investment cannot be examined.[2]

Yet, models without adjustment costs can be used to examine the effects of uncertainty on other aspects of firms' behaviour, such as optimal input choices and optimal output. This subsection deals with the impact of uncertainty on optimal production, whereas effects of uncertainty on input choices are considered in subsection 4.2.3.

Leland (1972) and Sandmo (1971) are two well known examples of studies examining the effects of uncertainty in the framework of the static firm model. They consider the effects of uncertainty on the optimal output and optimal price setting of the firm. Leland examines the effect of demand uncertainty. He shows that the impact of uncertainty crucially depends on the firm's mode of behaviour and attitude towards risk. Concerning the firm's mode of behaviour, the most extreme cases are monopolistic price setting and quantity setting behaviour, assuming a perfectly competitive firm. This difference is far more important under uncertainty than under certainty since under uncertainty some decisions have to be made before the stochastic term is known; in this literature these conditions are called *ex ante* controls. For instance, if the firm is a purely competitive quantity setter, output is an *ex ante* control, whereas price and actual sales are *ex post* controls since they are determined after the stochastic term is known. Leland shows that for a quantity setting firm faced with demand uncertainty, optimal output will be lower than the optimal output under certainty if the firm is risk averse. The opposite holds for a risk loving firm, whereas there is no effect on output for a risk neutral firm. Sandmo (1971) obtains the same result for a firm confronted with price uncertainty. He shows that for a risk averse firm faced with price uncertainty, output is smaller than the certainty output.

The following example, taken from McKenna (1986, p. 46-8) clarifies why optimal output for a risk averse competitive firm faced with uncertainty will be lower than output under certainty. McKenna considers a perfectly competitive firm that is a price taker and that is confronted with market price uncertainty. The market prices p are distributed according to a known probability distribution, $f(p)$. The firm maximizes the expected utility of profits, π, formulated as:

$$U(\pi) = \int u(pQ - v(Q) - a)f(p)dp \qquad (4.8)$$

where, in addition to the variables defined above, $v(Q)$ are variable costs ($v'(Q) > 0$) and a are fixed costs. It should be noted that since the firm is assumed to optimize the utility of profits, risk averse and risk loving behaviour should be taken into account (see the Appendix B on the relationship between utility functions and risk behaviour).

The first-order condition with respect to Q reads:

$$\int u'(\pi) \left[p - v'(Q) \right] f(p)dp \qquad (4.9)$$

Equation (4.9) can be rewritten as:

$$v'(Q^*) = \frac{\int u'(\pi^*)pf(p)dp}{\int u'(\pi^*)f(p)dp} \qquad (4.10)$$

where π^* means π evaluated at $Q = Q^*$ and where Q^* is optimal production. Under certainty the well known equality between price and marginal costs holds:

$$v'(Q') = p^a = \int pf(p)dp \qquad (4.11)$$

where p^a is the known market price under certainty, equal to the mean price under uncertainty, and Q' is the solution of the certainty case. For the certainty case a standard result is that at $Q = Q'$, and that marginal costs are increasing $(v''(Q') > 0)$. Assuming identical cost functions, this implies that $Q' > Q^*$ if $v'(Q') > v'(Q^*)$. Hence, $Q^* < Q'$ if:

$$v'(Q') > v'(Q^*) \qquad (4.12)$$

Therefore:

$$\int pf(p)dp > \frac{\int u'(\pi^*)pf(p)dp}{\int u'(\pi^*)f(p)dp} \qquad (4.13)$$

Equation (4.13) can be rewritten as:

$$0 > \frac{\int u'(\pi^*)pf(p)dp - p^a \int u'(\pi^*)f(p)dp}{\int u'(\pi^*)f(p)dp} = \frac{\int u'(\pi^*)(p-p^a)f(p)dp}{\int u'(\pi^*)f(p)dp} \qquad (4.14)$$

Therefore $Q^* < Q'$ if:

$$0 > \int u'(\pi^*)(p - p^a)f(p)dp \qquad (4.15)$$

Next, it will be shown that Equation (4.15) holds for a risk averse firm. For a risk averse firm $u''(\pi) < 0$, so that $u'(\pi) < u'(\pi^a)$ when $\pi > \pi^a$. π^a are known profits under certainty (mean profits under uncertainty). Note that $\pi > \pi^a$ when $p > p^a$. Hence, $p^a < p$ implies $u'(\pi) < u'(\pi^a)$. Define λ by:

$$\lambda = [u'(\pi^a) - u'(\pi)] (p - p^a) \qquad (4.16)$$

The sign of λ helps to prove Equation (4.15). Since $\lambda = 0$ for $p = p^a$. Differentiating λ with respect to p and p^a with $u'(\pi^a)$ constant gives:

$$\lambda'(p) = -u''(\pi)(p - p^a) + \left[u'(\pi^a) - u'(\pi)\right] \qquad (4.17)$$

Since $u''(\pi) < 0$ and $u'(\pi) < u'(\pi^a)$ in the case where $p^a < p$, it follows that $\lambda' > 0$ if $p > p^a$. Following the same line of reasoning it can be easily shown that $\lambda' < 0$ for $p < p^a$. Hence, λ is always positive except when $p = p^a$. From Equation (4.16) it now follows that:

$$u'(\pi^a)(p - p^a) > u'(\pi)(p - p^a) \qquad (4.18)$$

If we take expectations of both sides we get:

$$E[u'(\pi^a)(p - p^a)] > E[u'(\pi)(p - p^a)] \qquad (4.19)$$

Remember that $u'(\pi^a)$ is constant, so that this equation can be rewritten as:

$$u'(\pi^a) \int (p - p^a)f(p)dp > \int u'(\pi)(p - p^a)f(p)dp \qquad (4.20)$$

Since:

$$\int (p - p^a)f(p)dp = \int pf(p)dp - p^a = 0 \qquad (4.21)$$

it follows that:

$$0 > \int u'(\pi)(p - p^a)f(p)dp \qquad (4.22)$$

Equation (4.22) is exactly the same as condition (4.15). Hence, production by a risk averse perfectly competitive firm faced with price uncertainty is lower than production of a risk averse perfectly competitive firm producing under certainty and faced with the same mean price.

4.2.3 Effects of Sales Uncertainty on Optimal Input Choice: The Holthausen Model

Many authors have examined the effects of uncertainty on the optimal input choice and production. The main question in these studies is whether the deterministic rule for cost minimization, stating that a firm should employ capital and labour in such an amount that the marginal rate of substitution between the inputs equals the ratio of their prices, still holds under uncertainty. Holthausen (1976), Hartman (1976) and Das (1980) are well known examples of such studies.

The Holthausen model (1976) is a seminal example of this type of model.

It assumes that the firm is uncertain about the total demand for its goods. Yet, the firm's expectations of sales can be summarized in a subjective probability distribution. Following Leland (1972) an implicit demand relationship can be derived, which is specified as follows:

$$f(p,Q,u) = 0 \qquad (4.23)$$

where u is a random term. It is assumed that the price p and demand Q are inversely related for each level of u, and that an increase in u is associated with greater demand. If f has continuous partial derivatives, f can be solved for Q or p. If it is solved for p, the firm is assumed to be a quantity setter; if it is solved for Q, the firm is assumed to be a price setter.

A crucial assumption in this model is that labour is completely variable and therefore will always be set after demand is known, whereas capital is assumed to be quasi fixed. This is taken into account by assuming that the capital input is chosen before actual demand is observed. In the terminology of Leland, capital is an *ex ante* control, whereas labour is an *ex post* control. This assumption is also made by Das (1980) and Hartman (1976) but contrasts with the contributions of Leland (1972) and Sandmo (1971). To simplify the analysis, labour demand is not considered as a decision variable but is taken into account implicitly by a labour requirements function which guarantees that actual demand can always be fulfilled.

Holthausen shows that for the competitive and quantity setting firm the deterministic rule for cost minimization is not affected by uncertainty. The reason is that the firm sets output before the random demand is known and thus can choose the level of both inputs in line with the deterministic cost minimization rule. However, this does not imply that a firm faced with uncertainty uses the same level of labour and capital as a firm under certainty since, as shown in the previous section, optimal output for a competitive firm faced with uncertainty will most likely be lower than output under certainty. The result implies that the cost minimization rule as such is not affected by uncertainty.

A more interesting result can be derived for a price setter. The well known duality between profit maximization and cost minimization does not hold for a price setting non-risk neutral firm confronted with demand uncertainty: assuming price setting behaviour implies that the demand function can be written as:

$$Q = Q(p,u) \qquad (4.24)$$

where $Q_p < 0$ and $Q_u > 0$. The firm is assumed to optimize the utility of profits (π):

$$\max_{p,k} E[U(\pi)] \qquad (4.25)$$

Profits are defined by:

$$\pi = pQ(p,u) - p_k iK - wL(Q(p,u)) \tag{4.26}$$

where $L(Q(p,u))$ is the so-called labour requirement function. The decision variables are the price level and the capital stock. For our purpose the first order condition with respect to capital is relevant. It reads as:

$$E\left[U'(\pi)\left(-w\frac{\partial L(Q,k)}{\partial k} - p_k i\right)\right] = 0 \tag{4.27}$$

Since for two random variables $E[X,Y] = E[X]E[Y] + cov(X,Y)$, the above condition can be rewritten as:

$$EU'(\pi)E\left[-w\frac{\partial L(Q,k)}{\partial k} - p_k i\right] + w.cov\left(-\frac{\partial L(Q,k)}{\partial k}, -U'(\pi)\right) = 0 \tag{4.28}$$

so that:

$$E\left[-\frac{\partial L(Q,k)}{\partial k}\right] = \frac{p_k i}{w} - \frac{cov(-\frac{\partial L(Q,k)}{\partial k}, -U'(\pi))}{E[U'(\pi)]} \tag{4.29}$$

The deterministic rule for cost minimization implies that the marginal rate of substitution between capital and labour equals the inverse of their price ratio. Hence, the demand for capital is larger (smaller) than the amount of capital the firm uses if expected costs are minimized for a given level of output in the case were the left hand side of the above expression is smaller (larger) than $p_k i/w$. Since $U'(\pi) > 0$, the demand for capital will be above (below) the cost minimizing amount when the covariance term is positive (negative). Holthausen shows that under reasonable assumptions the covariance term is positive for risk loving firms, negative for risk averse firms and zero for risk neutral firms.

4.3   ORTHODOX MODELS WITH ADJUSTMENT COSTS

The models in the previous section assume that the firm can instantaneously and costlessly adjust its capital stock. Thus, the firm's problem is a static problem, where the marginal product of capital is equated to the user cost of capital. The optimal investment decision can be made by ignoring the future. Obviously, this is not a very realistic description of investment. In order to derive a truly dynamic investment model assumptions of the instantaneous and costless adjustment of the capital stock should be dropped. In the literature, this is modelled by means of adjustment costs and/or irreversibility. The implications of adjustment costs is the subject matter of Section 4.3, leaving irreversibility to be discussed in the next section.

4.3.1   Adjustment Costs

Adjustment costs are costs associated with the sale, purchase and productive implementation of capital goods above the basic price. The existence of adjustment costs are usually justified by referring to the required reorganisation and additional training when new machines are introduced. The literature on investment is not entirely clear on the preferred specification of adjustment costs. If a firm considers an investment, it is faced with three types of costs (see Hamermesh and Pfann 1996, and Dixit and Pindyck, 1994 p. 383):

1.   symmetric and asymmetric convex costs;
2.   piecewise linear costs; and
3.   lump-sum costs.

Convex adjustment costs
The traditional, and best known, category of adjustment costs are the convex adjustment costs. They usually depend on the rate at which capital stock is changed and are assumed to be convex in investment, generally with a minimum of zero when investment equals zero. The convex functions imply that the adjustment costs increase at an ever increasing rate with the absolute size of the rate of (dis)investment. Hence, it is assumed that both investment and disinvestment are costly. In case of asymmetry, disinvestment is assumed to be more (or less) costly than investment. In the case of convex adjustment costs, the optimal rate of investment is determined by the point where the marginal cost of raising the speed of adjustment of capital to its desired level is equal to the marginal benefit.

Eisner and Strotz (1963) present two arguments for assuming convexity:

1.   if the firm increases demand for investment in a single period, pressure will be put on the supply of investment goods;
2.   there are increasing costs associated with integrating new equipment.

The most convenient specifications are convex functions that are homogeneous of degree 1 in both investment and the capital stock. For this type of adjustment functions it can be shown that marginal q can be proxied by average q, together with a constant return to scale production function. Well known examples of convex adjustment cost functions are the quadratic Summers (1981) model:

$$C(I_t,K_t) = \frac{\alpha}{2}\left[\left(\frac{I}{K}\right)_t - v\right]^2 K_t \tag{4.30}$$

the Hubbard *et al.* (1995) specification:

$$C(I_t,K_t) = \frac{\alpha}{2}\left[\left(\frac{I}{K}\right)_t - v\right] I_t \tag{4.31}$$

and the higher-power function as proposed by Whited (1995):

$$C(I_t,K_t) = \left(\alpha_0 + \sum_{m=2}^{M}\frac{1}{m}\alpha_m\left(\frac{1}{K}\right)^m\right) K_t \tag{4.32}$$

The latter function closely resembles the quadratic cost function for $M = 2$. $C(.,.)$ denotes the adjustment costs function. Equivalence implies $\alpha_0 = \frac{\alpha_2}{2}v^2 - \alpha_2 v\frac{I}{K}$. A typical asymmetric convex adjustment function is the one used by Pfann and Verspagen (1989):

$$C(I) = \frac{1}{2}\alpha_1 I^2 - \alpha_1 I + e^{\alpha_1 I} - 1 \tag{4.33}$$

Symmetry holds for $\alpha_1 = 0$. If $\alpha_1 > 0$, marginal cost of positive adjustment exceeds that of negative adjustment.

Piecewise linear costs
Firms may face costs that vary linearly with the amount of change in the capital stock. These primarily include the costs that have to be paid for the purchase of capital goods. Often there is an asymmetry in the sense that the purchase price of capital is assumed to be higher than the resale price. This type of adjustment function is often used to account for partially irreversible investment (see the next section). If both prices are the same, capital goods are fully reversible. However, a wedge between the purchase and sales price of capital can explain partial irreversibility. This wedge may be the result of transaction costs, installation costs, the firm-specific nature of capital, or adverse selection in the market for used capital goods. A resell price of zero corresponds with complete irreversibility. These costs vary linearly with the quantity of change in the capital stock but do not depend on the length of time over which the change is accomplished. An example of piecewise linear costs

is:

$$C(I,K) = [I > 0]\alpha_1 I + [I \le 0]\alpha_2 I \tag{4.34}$$

where $[I > 0]$ is an indicator function. α_1, α_2 need not have the same absolute value.

Lump-sum costs

If a firm alters its capital stock, there may be some lump-sum fixed costs. These costs are independent of the volume of investment but may or may not depend on the length of the period over which investment takes place. If they depend on the investment period, they are called *flow* fixed costs. If they do not depend on the investment period, they are called *stock* fixed costs. In the words of Caballero and Leahy (1996, p. 3) "stock fixed costs are the cost of turning on a tap independent of how much water flows through it or how long the water flows, whereas flow fixed costs are the costs of running the tap per unit of time water flows and is independent of how much water flows."

In the literature there are examples of cost functions that combine different forms of adjustment costs. A well known example is the cost function used by Caballero (1991), which is specified as:

$$C(I) = I + [I > 0]\gamma_1 I^\beta + [I < 0]\gamma_2 |I|^\beta \tag{4.35}$$

where $\beta \ge 1$, and γ_1 and γ_2 are two nonnegative parameters. In this cost function, the price of capital is set at 1. The cost function allows for direct cost (I) and symmetric convex cost $(\gamma_1 = \gamma_2 > 0)$. The cost function implies irreversible investment when $\gamma_1 = 0$ and $\gamma_2 = \infty$ and $\beta = 1$.

A most complete model of adjustment costs has been constructed by Abel and Eberly (1994). They present a model in which all of the above mentioned costs, except for stock fixed costs are taken into account.[3] Their cost function not only includes the traditional convex adjustment costs, it also includes costs that may explain irreversibility. More specifically, they argue that a firm faces three types of costs when it invests.

1. Purchase or sale costs; these are the piecewise linear costs of buying or selling uninstalled capital.

2. Adjustment costs: these depend on the rate at which the capital stock is being changed; this is the traditional category of convex adjustment costs.

3. Fixed costs of investment, which have a fixed character and are independent of the level of investment.

Once an action is taken, the new capital good creates a flow of fixed costs. The total cost function is continuous, strictly convex and twice differentiable with respect to investment I, except at $I = 0$. If investment goes to (minus) infinity the limit of the cost function also reaches (minus) infinity. The total costs equal the product of a dummy variable (v) and the extended cost function. The dummy variable takes the value 0 when investment is 0. Hence, the total cost function reads $vC(I,K)$ where $v = 0$ when $I = 0$ and $v = 1$ in all other cases.

The situation with $I = 0$ is the interesting case. The limits of the cost function $C(.,.)$ for I approaching 0 from positive and negative values is the same and labelled $C(0,K)$. This is the fixed nonnegative cost of investment. The left and right hand derivatives of the cost function with respect to investment I evaluated at $I = 0$ are unequal, though. It is assumed that the right hand derivative is nonnegative and larger or equal than the left hand partial derivative.

4.3.2 Risk Neutral Firms and Uncertainty in All Periods: The Hartman Model

After this short digression on adjustment costs, we proceed by presenting the most important contributions to the investment uncertainty literature. Probably one of the first dynamic adjustment cost investment models that included uncertainty is the model by Hartman (1972). Hartman considers a perfectly competitive risk neutral firm with a constant returns to scale production function and with convex adjustment costs. He examines the effects of uncertainty with respect to future wages (w) and future goods prices (p).

The adjustment cost function has the following properties: for $I > 0, C'(I) > 0$; for $I < 0, C'(I) < 0$ and for $I = 0, C'(I) = 0$. Moreover, $C''(I) > 0$. These properties imply that adjustment costs increase with the absolute size of investment or disinvestment, that adjustment costs are zero when gross investment is zero, and that adjustment costs rise at an ever increasing rate.

The firm is assumed to be risk neutral and maximizes the expected present value of cash flows:

$$V = E \int_0^\infty \left[p_t F(K_t, L_t) - w_t L_t - p_{k,t} I_t - C(I_t) \right] e^{-\rho t} dt \qquad (4.36)$$

subject to the capital accumulation equation:

$$\frac{dK}{dt} = I_t - \delta K_t \qquad (4.37)$$

Hartman shows that the first-order condition for the firm under uncertainty becomes the equality between the marginal adjustment cost and the *expected* present value of the net return on the marginal unit of capital. In general, the outcome is (see also Nickell, 1978, p. 29):

$$C'(I_t) = \int_t^\infty p_s F_K(K(s), L(s)) e^{-(\delta+\rho)(s-t)} ds - p_{k,t} \qquad (4.38)$$

The first term on the right hand side of this equation gives the present value at time t of additional revenue resulting from purchasing an extra unit of capital stock at time t. Note that capital purchased at time t not only provides additional income as given by the marginal revenue product in period t but does so until infinity. However, revenues in period s should be discounted in terms of period t units, and therefore must be multiplied by $e^{-\rho(s-t)}$. Moreover, it should be taken into account that the capital stock in period s should be corrected by a depreciation factor. An increase of one marginal unit of capital at time t increases the capital stock at time $s > t$ with $e^{-\delta(s-t)}$. Note that $e^{-\rho(s-t)} e^{-\delta(s-t)}$ equals $e^{-(\delta+\rho)(s-t)}$. The second term on the right hand side denotes the cost of purchasing one unit of capital. The optimal outcome results when the net gains from purchasing one unit of capital equals adjustment costs $C'(I_t)$. The condition is somewhat problematic since the additional revenues depend on the entire time path of the capital stock from period t until infinity, which depends on the current rate of investment. In other words, there are intertemporal links that make it difficult to solve the model.

The analysis becomes much more simple if constant returns to scale are assumed, as is the case in the Hartman model. With constant returns to scale, $F(K, L)$ may be rewritten as $Lf(k)$, where k is the capital labour ratio. Labour demand is given by the equality between the marginal revenue product of labour and the real wage rate. With constant returns to scale, this implies that:

$$f - \frac{k \partial f}{\partial k} = \frac{w}{p} \qquad (4.39)$$

Taking into account that the marginal revenue product of labour is increasing in k, this equation can be solved for the capital labour ratio:

$$k = g\left(\frac{w}{p}\right); g' > 0 \qquad (4.40)$$

Hence, in each period the capital labour ratio is determined by the real wage rate. Since the marginal revenue product of capital can be written as $\partial f(k)/\partial k =$

f_k, Equation (4.38) can be rewritten as:

$$C'(I_t) = \int_t^\infty p_s \frac{\partial F}{\partial K} f_k \left(\frac{w_s}{p_s} \right) e^{-(\delta+\rho)(s-t)} ds - p_{k,t} \qquad (4.41)$$

Thus, the marginal revenue product of capital and therefore also investment becomes a function of prices only. Most importantly, intertemporal links in the sense that investment now depends on the capital stock of tomorrow, which in turn depends on the current rate of investment, do not exist anymore. In the next section we will show the implications which this has for the effects of uncertainty on investment. In discrete time Equation (4.41) can be written as (see Nickell, 1978, p. 94):

$$C'(I_t) = \sum_{s=t}^\infty \alpha(s,t) E \left[p_s f_k \left(\frac{w_s}{p_s} \right) \right] - p_{k,t} \qquad (4.42)$$

where $\alpha(s,t)$ is the discount factor. The effect of uncertain goods prices and wages becomes clear by considering $p_s f_k(\frac{w_s}{p_s})$. Jensen's inequality (see Appendix B) implies that an increase in price or wage uncertainty leads to an increase in the expected value of the marginal productivity of capital $E \left[p_s f_k(\frac{w_s}{p_s}) \right]$ in the case where the marginal revenue product of capital is a convex function of w and p. For an optimum outcome this implies that $C'(I_t)$ also increases and that I increases also. Since the marginal revenue product of capital is always convex in both the price and wage rate for a constant returns to scale production function (see again Nickell, 1978, p. 112-13), an increase in price uncertainty in any future period stimulates investment in the Hartman model (1972).

4.3.3 Risk Neutral Firms and Future Uncertainty only: The Abel Model

In the models that have been examined so far, it is assumed that there is uncertainty in some future period, as well as in the current period. Pindyck (1982), Abel (1983) and many of their successors use a different stochastic specification. They assume that there is only future uncertainty and that all current variables are known. More specifically, they assume that the stochastic variable follows a (generalization of a) Wiener process (see Appendix C). These authors claim that this assumption is more in line with reality, since in practice firms face much more uncertainty regarding future events than in the current period.

The models of Pindyck and Abel, in line with Hartman (1972), deal with a risk neutral competitive firm that is faced with price (and demand) uncertainty. Pindyck shows that an increase in price uncertainty will reduce the rate of investment if adjustment costs are concave. Only in the case where adjustment costs are convex will an increase in price uncertainty lead to an increase in the investment rate. This result differs completely from the Hartman (1972) result. Hartman shows that an increase in price uncertainty will increase the investment rate if the production function is linearly homogeneous, and therefore the marginal revenue product of capital is a strictly convex function of the price of output, irrespective of the adjustment function. However, Abel (1983) correctly criticizes the solution method used by Pindyck. Pindyck solves his model by comparing a phase diagram for a stochastic and nonstochastic version of his model. In the phase diagrams there is a stationary locus in which the (expected) rate of change of investment is zero. Abel argues that the use of a phase diagram in the stochastic case is not valid. He states that there is no reason that the firm is on the expectational stationary locus for investment and thus that the expected rate of change of investment is eventually zero. Moreover, he shows that in the presence of uncertainty, the expected growth rate of investment is in general not equal to zero so that Pindyck's analysis is not suitable. In terms of the phase diagram, Abel's remarks imply that the stationary locus for the expected rate of change of investment exhibits drift due to the stochastic behaviour of variables other than the variables on the axes of the phase diagram.

Abel reformulates the model of Pindyck and explicitly solves it without relying on phase diagrams. He assumes that the firm optimizes the present value of cash flows, subject to the capital accumulation equation and the stochastic process of the price of output. In line with Hartman, he also uses a constant returns to scale production function. The model's objective function is:

$$V(K_t, p_t) = \max_{I_s, L_s} E_t \int_t^\infty \left[p_s L_s^\alpha K_s^{1-\alpha} - wL_s - \gamma I_s^\beta \right] e^{(-\rho(s-t))} ds \qquad (4.43)$$

subject to

$$dK_t = (I_t - \delta K_t) \, dt \qquad (4.44)$$

$$dp_t / p_t = \sigma dz \qquad (4.45)$$

where $\beta > 1$ is the constant elasticity of the cost of investment and dz is a Wiener process with mean zero and unit variance. The price process has the properties that $E_t(p_s) = p_t$, $s \geq t$ and the variance of p_s equals $(s - t)\sigma^2$. Abel solves the above problem by using the technique of Dynamic Programming. [4] The Bellman equation (see Appendix C) for this problem is:

$$\rho V(k_t, p_t) dt = \max_{I_t, L_t} \left[p_t L_t^\alpha K_t^{1-\alpha} - wL_t - \gamma I_t^\beta \right] dt + E_t[dV] \qquad (4.46)$$

The next step in the solution is the calculation of the expected capital gain

$(E_t[dV])$. The value of the firm depends on the state variables K and p. Since p follows a Wiener process, Ito's lemma (see Appendix C) is needed to calculate dV. Taking a second order Taylor expansion of $V(p,K)$ gives:

$$dV = V_K dK + V_p dp + \frac{1}{2} V_{KK}(dK)^2 + \frac{1}{2} V_{pp}(dp)^2 + V_{pk}(dp)(dK) \qquad (4.47)$$

Substituting the two equations of motion for dK_t and dp_t:

$$E[dV] = V_K(I_t - \delta K_t)\,dt + V_p p_t \sigma dz + \frac{1}{2} V_{KK}((I_t - \delta K_t)\,dt)^2$$
$$+ \frac{1}{2} V_{pp}(p_t \sigma dz)^2 + V_{pk}(p_t \sigma dz)((I_t - \delta K_t)\,dt) \qquad (4.48)$$

According to the rules of multiplication for Wiener terms (see Appendix C) $(dt)^2 = (dt)(dz) = dz = 0$ and $(dz)^2 = dt$ and therefore:

$$E[dV] = \left[V_K(I_t - \delta K_t) + \frac{1}{2} V_{pp} p_t^2 \sigma^2 \right] dt \qquad (4.49)$$

The Bellman equation can now be rewritten as:

$$\rho V(k_t, p_t) = \max_{I_t, L_t} \left[p_t L_t^\alpha K_t^{1-\alpha} - wL_t - \gamma I_t^\beta + V_K(I_t - \delta K_t) + \frac{1}{2} V_{pp} p_t^2 \sigma^2 \right] \qquad (4.50)$$

The demand for labour can be derived by differentiating the right hand side with respect to L. This gives:

$$L_t = \left(\frac{w}{\alpha p_t} \right)^{1/(\alpha-1)} K_t \qquad (4.51)$$

By substituting the demand for labour on the right hand side of the Bellman equation it can be shown that:

$$\max_{L_t} \left[p_t L_t^\alpha K_t^{1-\alpha} - wL_t \right] = (1-\alpha)\left(\frac{\alpha}{w}\right)^{\alpha/(1-\alpha)} p_t^{1/(1-\alpha)} K_t = h p_t^{1/(1-\alpha)} K_t \qquad (4.52)$$

An investment function can be derived by differentiating the right hand side of the Bellman equation with respect to I:

$$\gamma \beta I_t^{\beta-1} = V_K \qquad (4.53)$$

Substituting the investment equation in the Bellman equation, taking into account Equation (4.52) gives:

$$\rho V(k_t, p_t) = h p_t^{1/(1-\alpha)} K_t + (\beta - 1)\gamma I_t^\beta - \delta K_t V_K + \frac{1}{2} V_{pp} p_t^2 \sigma^2 \qquad (4.54)$$

Equations (4.53) and (4.54) can be combined to form a second-order partial differential equation for the value function V. Abel shows that the solution equals:

$$V(K_t, p_t) = q_t K_t + \frac{(\beta - 1)\gamma (q_t/\beta\gamma)^{\beta/(\beta-1)}}{r - \frac{\beta(1-\alpha+\alpha\beta)\sigma^2}{2(1-\alpha)^2(\beta-1)^2}} \qquad (4.55)$$

where:

$$q = \frac{h p_t^{1/(1-\alpha)}}{r + \delta - \frac{\alpha\sigma^2}{2(1-\alpha)^2}} \qquad (4.56)$$

Since $I_t = (\frac{1}{\beta\gamma} V_K)^{1/\beta-1}$ it follows that:

$$I_t = \left(\frac{q_t}{\beta\gamma}\right)^{(1/\beta-1)} \qquad (4.57)$$

There are several important and interesting results. First, investment is a linear and increasing function of q, which can be shown to be equal to the expected marginal revenue product of capital; hence the model is consistent with the well known q models of investment.[5] Second, uncertainty affects investment only through q. Third, the effect of uncertainty on investment can be evaluated by considering the effects of uncertainty on q. It is obvious that an increase in price uncertainty, as measured by σ^2, leads to an increase in the marginal revenue product of capital and consequently to an increase in q and so to investment. Abel argues that this result will hold as long as the marginal revenue product of capital is a strictly convex function of the price of output. If this is the case, due to Jensen's inequality an increase in price uncertainty will always lead to an increase in the expected marginal revenue product of capital and consequently to investment. Hence Abel's results concerning the effects of uncertainty on investment are in agreement with the results of Hartman (1972) but they contradict Pindyck (1982) who only finds positive effects of uncertainty on investment if the adjustment function is convex.

4.3.4   Models with Risk Averse Firms: The Approach of Nickell

One of the main conclusions of the models by Hartman (1972) and Abel (1983) is that an increase in uncertainty stimulates investment if the marginal product of capital is a convex function in the variable of whose evolution is uncertain. This will always be the case for a perfectly competitive firm with a constant returns to scale production function. However, these papers assume that firms are risk neutral, and hence ignore the possible negative effects of uncertainty on investment through firms' risk aversion. Risk aversion can be taken into account by assuming that firms optimize the utility of profits. Alternatively, if firms optimize profits, risk aversion could be introduced by assuming that the rate of discount is not constant but is affected by changes in uncertainty.

There are a few papers that assume that the investment decision is made by risk averse agents. An exception is the model by Zeira (1990), who uses a very simple general overlapping generations model in which risk averse consumers decide to invest in either a risky or a riskless asset. It is assumed that young consumers allocate their savings between a pure capital technology or a capital-labour technology. Uncertainty enters the model through random wages, so that investing in the capital labour technology corresponds with investing in a risky asset. Zeira considers the effect of more uncertainty on the share of saving invested in the risky asset. He shows that an increase in uncertainty may lead to higher or lower investment in the risky asset, depending on the degree of risk aversion of consumers and the concavity of the production function in labour. If consumers are more risk averse, increased uncertainty will lead to a decline in investment. On the other hand, the more concave the production function is in labour, the more convex the profit function will be in wages; increased uncertainty has a positive effect on investment. Most importantly, the paper shows that uncertainty may have a negative effect on investment even when profits are convex in the variable of which the behaviour is uncertain.

Probably the most direct way to introduce risk averse behaviour of firms is to assume that firms optimize the expected utility of profits rather than to maximize profits itself. However, in a dynamic context the solutions of this type of problem become quite difficult. A way to overcome this difficulty is the approach originally developed by Stevens (1974) that was applied by Nickell (1978). He derives the value function of the firm by explicitly using the mean variance model. Assuming that both the future riskless interest rates and the market prices of risk are known with certainty, he shows that (for a risk averse firm) the value of firm i equals:

$$V_i(0) = \int_0^\infty \left(E[\pi_{it}] - m_t \left(var(\pi_{it}) + \sum_j cov(\pi_{it}, \pi_{jt}) \right) \right) e^{-\rho t} dt \qquad (4.58)$$

Hence, there are two additional terms: the variance of cash flow (dividends) and the covariance of cash flows. If it is assumed that firm i expects that future deviations in dividends of all firms are related, the above expression can be rewritten as (see Nickell, 1978, p. 163):

$$V_i(0) = \int_0^\infty \left(E[\pi_{it}] - n_t var(\pi_{it})\right) e^{-\rho t} dt \qquad (4.59)$$

where n_t will generally be positive (although it may be negative for firms that do well when most other firms do badly). A positive n_t may be seen as representing a risk averse objective function, whereas a negative n_t corresponds with risk loving behaviour.

Nickell applies this objective function to the Hartman model (1972) in which prices and wages are uncertain. By taking into account that labour input is chosen when prices are certain, cash flow in the Hartman model can be rewritten as:

$$\pi = g(p.w)K - p_k I - C(I) \qquad (4.60)$$

with

$$g(p.w)K = \max_L \left(pF(K,L) - wL\right) \qquad (4.61)$$

where g is convex in p and w. The value of the firm can now be written as:

$$V_j(0) = \int_0^\infty \left[K_t E[g(p,w)] - p_{k,t} I_t - C(I_t) - nK_t^2 var\, g(p,w)\right] e^{-\rho s} dt \qquad (4.62)$$

The optimality condition becomes (see Nickell, 1978, p.164):

$$C'(I_s) = \int_s^\infty \left[E[g(p,w)] - 2nK_t var\, g(p,w)\right] e^{-(\delta+\rho)(t-s)} dt - p_{k,s} \qquad (4.63)$$

The optimality condition in the original Hartman model, Equation (4.41), can be rewritten by using Equation (4.61). This gives:

$$C'(I_s) = \int_s^\infty E[g(p,w)e^{-(\delta+\rho)(t-s)} dt] - p_{k,s} \qquad (4.64)$$

Since C' is increasing in I, the rate of investment using the objective function proposed by Nickell is lower than the optimal rate of investment using the Hartman *risk neutral* objective function as long as $n > 0$ or, in other words, as long as firms are risk averse. Hence, this approach may lead to a negative influence of uncertainty on investment.

4.4 CONCLUSIONS

This chapter reviews orthodox studies on investment and uncertainty. The orthodox models assume that the investment decision is a decision that has to be taken at a particular moment in time. We distinguish between models with and without adjustment costs. Models without adjustment costs are static and are in fact not real investment models; therefore, the effects of uncertainty on investment cannot be considered in these models. Hence, the effects of uncertainty on production and the optimal input choice are considered. It is shown that for a risk averse firm optimal output is lower in the presence of uncertainty than under certainty. Concerning the optimal input choice, it is shown that the deterministic rule for cost minimization is not affected by uncertainty when the firm is perfectly competitive. However, for an imperfectly competitive firm, the duality between profit maximization and cost minimization no longer holds. For risk loving (averse) firms the capital labour ratio will be higher (lower) than the optimal level derived from cost minimization.

Turning to models with adjustment costs, we distinguish between models assuming risk neutrality and risk aversion. We show that a competitive, risk neutral firm is positively affected by uncertainty as long as the marginal productivity of capital is a convex function of prices, which will be the case for a constant returns to scale production function. On the other hand, if a firm is risk averse, or if the marginal productivity is concave in the variable whose evolution is uncertain, an increase in uncertainty may have a negative effect on investment.

NOTES

1. This is also a result of the implicit assumption of perfect capital markets.
2. Jorgenson circumvents this problem by assuming that the actual capital stock gradually moves to the optimal capital stock K^*, hence:

$$I_t = j[K^* - K_t] \qquad (4.65)$$

Thus he also prevents the model from making vertical jumps in the capital stock that are not allowed in the dynamic representation of his model.
3. Caballero and Leahy (1996) consider stock fixed costs and show that the traditional q theory of investment breaks down with stock fixed costs.
4. This model can also be solved by using the Lagrange method, see Chow (1997, Chapter 8).
5. Marginal q equals the marginal benefit of capital when the price of capital goods is set to unity, as is the case in the Abel model.

5. The Option Approach to Investment under Uncertainty

5.1 INTRODUCTION

Chapter 4 has shown that investment by a competitive risk-neutral firm is positively affected by uncertainty as long as the marginal productivity of capital is a convex function of prices. This will be the case for a constant returns to scale production function. If a firm is risk averse or if marginal productivity is concave in the variable of which the development is uncertain, an increase in uncertainty may have a negative effect on investment. However, there is another way in which uncertainty may have a negative effect on investment, and this has to do with the effect of uncertainty on the timing of investment. Uncertainty may have a negative effect on investment since it may lead to a delay in the investment decision. This effect is ignored by orthodox investment theories but it is one of the key issues in new investment theories.

Orthodox investment theories assume that the investment decision is to be taken now or never. However, it may be profitable for firms to wait for more information on the state of the world relevant to the project, especially when investments are (partly) irreversible. Due to a lack of realism of the underlying assumptions and especially due to the poor empirical behaviour of orthodox investment theories, a new approach to investment under uncertainty has recently been developed. This new view emphasizes three important characteristics of investment (Dixit and Pindyck, 1994). First, investment is (partly) irreversible, implying that there are sunk costs of investment that cannot be completely recovered by selling capital. Second, investment decisions have to be made in an uncertain world. Third, it is possible to delay the investment decision in order to obtain more information about the future.

Section 5.2 gives an example of how uncertainty may cause a decline in immediate investment, even for risk neutral firms, if irreversibility is taken into account. Sections 5.3, 5.4, 5.5 and 5.6 survey the contributions by McDonald and Siegel (1986), Bertola (1998), Caballero (1991), Abel *et al.* (1996), and Sarkar (2000) respectively. Section 5.8 concludes this chapter. Appendix C provides some mathematical details.

5.2   A BASIC EXAMPLE

The new approach to investment under uncertainty makes an analogy between the real investment decision and a financial call option and hence is called the option approach to investment. A call option gives an investor the right during a certain period to buy an asset for a predetermined price (the *exercise* price). Once the asset is bought, the option is irreversible, implying that the moment at which the option is exercised is extremely important. The similarity with a real investment decision is clear. An investor, having the opportunity to invest and being uncertain about the future developments of key variables that affect the profitability of a project, may decide to wait for more relevant information and hence may decide to delay investment. The investor controls the timing of the investment. The optimal outcome is characterized by the equality between the value of waiting for new information and the opportunity costs of postponing the investment in terms of foregone returns.

Real option theory implies that the standard net present value rule for investment, stating that investment should take place until the value of capital equals the purchase costs, has to be modified by taking into account the fact that once the investment has been made the option to invest no longer exists. In other words: investors need to be compensated for the loss in value related to the disappearance of the investment option when the investment has been exercised. This implies that a firm should only invest once the anticipated return exceeds the purchase costs plus the option value to wait. Recent literature emphasizes that especially in an uncertain environment the option value to wait can be substantial. This provides another argument why uncertainty may cause a decline in immediate investment, even for risk neutral firms.

A simple example taken from Serven (1997) may illustrate. Consider a risk neutral firm that decides on an irreversible investment project. The investment costs (purchase costs) are p_k, and the discount rate is ρ. At period $t = 0$ there is a single state with a known return at the end of the year of R_0. From period $t = 1$ onwards there is an uncertain return with an expected value $E_0[R]$. If the firm invests in period $t = 0$, the present value of expected cash flows (V_0) is:

$$
\begin{aligned}
V_0 &= -p_k + \frac{1}{1+\rho}R_0 + \left(\frac{1}{1+\rho}\right)^2 \sum_{t=0}^{\infty}(1+\rho)^{-t}E_0[R] \\
&= -p_k + (1+\rho)^{-1}[R_0 + (1/\rho)E_0[R]]
\end{aligned}
\tag{5.1}
$$

According to the traditional approach a firm will invest as long as $V_0 > 0$.

Rewriting equation (5.1), this implies that a firm should invest if:

$$\frac{(1+\rho)^{-1}[R_0 + (1/\rho)E_0[R]]}{p_k} = q > 1 \tag{5.2}$$

where q is marginal q, measured as the present discounted value of future profits over the purchase cost. Alternatively, equation (5.1) implies that a firm should invest if:

$$(R_0 - \rho p_k) + \frac{(E_0[R] - \rho p_k)}{\rho} > 0 \tag{5.3}$$

where ρp_k can be seen as the user cost of capital. In the case where investment is fully reversible, future decisions can always be undone. This implies that the future becomes unimportant so that the second term can be ignored and a firm should invest only if current returns exceed the user costs of capital ($R_0 > \rho p_k$).

However, if the firm has an opportunity to wait the above calculations ignore a cost, since by investing the firm gives up the option of waiting and hence loses the option to invest. The above decision rule may become inappropriate, e.g. if a firm makes an irreversible commitment, and there is a chance that $R < \rho p_k$ so that the future return is less than total costs. It may then pay to delay the investment decision in order to learn more about future returns.

Assume that after one period there is no longer uncertainty and that future returns remain constant at the realized value of next year. If the firm waits for one period and only invests if the return exceeds the purchase costs, the expected present value of cash flows becomes (V_1):

$$V_1 = \Pr[R > \rho p_k] \left(\frac{1}{1+\rho}(-p_k) + \left[\frac{1}{1+\rho}\right]^2 \sum_{t=0}^{\infty} (1+\rho)^{-t} E_0[R|R > \rho p_k] \right) \tag{5.4}$$

$Pr[A > B]$ denotes the probability that $A > B$. By using:

$$E_0[R] = \Pr[R > \rho p_k] E_0[R|R > \rho p_k] + \Pr[R \le \rho p_k] E_0[R|R \le \rho p_k] \tag{5.5}$$

it can be derived that:

$$V_1 - V_0 = F = \left(\frac{1}{1+\rho}\right) \left[\Pr[R < \rho p_k] \frac{E_0[\rho p_k - R|R < \rho p_k]}{\rho} - (R_0 - \rho p_k) \right] \tag{5.6}$$

where F is the option value of waiting. If $F < 0$, the firm should invest immediately; if not, the firm should wait one period. By rewriting the above equation it can be shown that a firm should invest immediately if:

$$(R - \rho p_k) > \Pr[R < \rho p_k] \frac{E_0[\rho p_k - R | R < \rho p_k]}{\rho} \tag{5.7}$$

The interpretation of Equation (5.7) is straightforward: a firm should invest immediately only if the opportunity costs of waiting, *i.e.* the foregone returns of not investing immediately $(R - \rho p_k)$, exceed the value of waiting. The value of waiting is given by the irreversible mistake which the firm would make by immediately investing when project returns are below user costs of capital. This mistake is made with probability $\Pr[R < \rho p_k]$ and accrues each period until infinity, so that it has to be divided by ρ in order to convert it into present value terms. Note that the value of waiting should be calculated in period $t = 0$ expected value terms. The above expression shows that the firm should decide to invest immediately only if the first period return exceeds the user cost of capital by an amount that compensates for the possible irreversibility costs of being committed to an unprofitable project. It is also clear that the critical first period return that warrants immediate investment depends only on *bad* news, represented by a future realisation of R below ρp_k. It is not affected by good news, as proxied by a future realization of R larger than ρp_k. This is the *bad news principle*, originally formulated by Bernanke (1983). The reason is that waiting depends on the ability to avoid the consequences of *bad* news rather than of *good* news. The consequence of the bad news principle is that generally any increase in downside risk increases the option value of waiting and hence (*ceteris paribus*) would lead to a decline in immediate investment.

Before concluding this section, it should be noted that the option approach does not imply that uncertainty always has a negative effect on investment by risk neutral firms. This depends on two opposing effects. First, the above analysis implies that an increase in uncertainty raises the investment hurdle, *i.e.* the minimum required return which a firm expects to earn for an immediate investment. Hence, this effect would imply that more uncertainty negatively affects investment. Second, as shown in the previous sections, an increase in uncertainty leads to an increase in expected profitability and consequently in investment when the marginal revenue product is a convex function of the uncertain variable (mostly prices). This latter effect is ignored by the example in this section where marginal returns were assumed to be given. In reality, this effect would still hold so that the impact of higher uncertainty on investment depends on whether the threshold or the marginal revenue effect dominates.

5.3 THE OPTIMAL TIMING OF AN INVESTMENT PROJECT

One of the first models of irreversible investment that uses the option approach to investment is developed by McDonald and Siegel (1986). They show that investment irreversibility and uncertainty drives a wedge between the value of the project (value of a unit capital) and investment costs. Moreover, by deriving an exact expression for the wedge they are able to show to what extent the net present value rule has to be adjusted. Since the McDonald and Siegel model gives a simple formalization to the roles played by irreversibility and delay, this model will be discussed in more detail. The analysis of a somewhat simplified version of the McDonald and Siegel model as given by Dixit and Pindyck (1994, Chapter 5) will be followed.

McDonald and Siegel examine the investment timing problem of a firm. The firm controls the timing of a totally irreversible investment and in each period choses between investing (stopping) or waiting one more period (continuation). The model analyses when the firm should pay a sunk cost I in order to obtain an investment value V, where V is uncertain in future periods. If the firm decides not to wait longer, the firm obtains the termination payoff which is equal to the project value minus the sunk investment costs. The investment costs of the project I are assumed to be constant. The present value of the expected future cash flows, *i.e.* the value of the project, is assumed to follow a geometric Brownian motion with drift (see Appendix C):

$$\frac{dV}{V} = \alpha_v dt + \sigma_v dz_v \tag{5.8}$$

where dz_v is an increment of a Wiener process. This assumption implies that the present value of the project is known when the firm invests immediately. However, when the firm invests, the future value becomes uncertain with a variance that grows linearly with the time horizon. The equation shows that there is a growth effect, represented by a positive α_v and an uncertainty effect given by σ_v. The assumption that the value of the project follows a Brownian motion is made for the sake of simplicity. It may well be the case that the value of the project does not follow a Brownian motion but follows another stochastic process. Moreover, the change in the value of the project is caused by changes in the underlying variables, such as prices, wages and sales. A much better approach would be to explicitly model the sources of value fluctuations, possible by means of Wiener processes. This, however, becomes more complicated and often becomes unmanageable; see Dixit and Pindyck (1994) for several extensions of the basic McDonald and Siegel (1986) model.

The payoff from investing at time t is $V_t - I$. The problem is to maximize:

$$X(V) = \max E\,[V_t - I]\,e^{-\rho t} \tag{5.9}$$

subject to Equation (5.8). $X(V)$ denotes the value of the option to invest. E denotes the expectation operator, ρ is a constant discount rate, and t is the unknown future date of the investment. It is assumed that $\alpha_v < \rho$, since otherwise waiting would always be better than investing and V would increase indefinitely as a function of t. Note that the existence of an option value to invest is the direct consequence of the assumed (complete) irreversibility and the possibility to delay. The equivalence with a call option with no expiration date should now be clear: the firm has the right to undertake the project at a prespecified price I. The firm wants to optimize the value of the investment opportunity. [1]

The problem is to find a critical value labelled V^* such that firms will invest once $V > V^*$. Dixit and Pindyck solve this problem by using both Dynamic Programming and contingent claims analysis. Here the dynamic programming solution is used. The first step is to formulate the Bellman equation for the continuation regime. In Appendix C a general expression of the Bellman equation for dynamic investment problems is derived (see Equation (C.26)). If it is taken into account that the immediate payoff is zero since the investment only yields cash after it has taken place, the Bellman equation for values of V at which the firm should not yet invest becomes:

$$\rho X(V_t)dt = E[dX] \tag{5.10}$$

The next step is to calculate the expected capital gain $E[dX]$. The value of the firm depends on the state variable, V, which follows a Wiener process so that Ito's lemma (see Appendix C) is needed to calculate dX. Taking a second order Taylor expansion of $X(V)$ gives:

$$dX = X_V dV + \frac{1}{2}X_{VV}(dV)^2 \tag{5.11}$$

Substitution of the equation of motion for dV and taking the expectation gives:

$$E[dX] = X_V V\,(\alpha_v dt + \sigma_v dz_v) + \frac{1}{2}X_{VV}(\alpha_v V dt + \sigma_v V dz_v)^2 \tag{5.12}$$

According to the rules of multiplication for Wiener terms (see Appendix C):

$(dt)^2 = (dt)(dz_v) = dz_v = 0$ and $(dz_v)^2 = dt$, and hence:

$$E[dX] = \alpha_v V X_V dt + \frac{1}{2}\sigma_v^2 V^2 X_{VV} dt \qquad (5.13)$$

The Bellman equation can now be rewritten as:

$$\frac{1}{2}\sigma_v^2 V^2 X_{VV} + \alpha_v V X_V - \rho X = 0 \qquad (5.14)$$

This equation is a second order differential equation. It must be solved subject to following three boundary conditions (see also the Appendix C):

$$X(0) = 0 \qquad (5.15)$$
$$X(V^*) = V^* - I \qquad (5.16)$$
$$X'(V^*) = 1 \qquad (5.17)$$

Equation (5.15) holds since the option to invest will have no value when V approaches zero. Equation (5.16) is the value matching condition, stating that on the boundary the firm gets $V^* - I$ when it invests. Equation (5.17) is the smooth-pasting condition, which implies that $X(V)$ is continuous at the threshold of V^*.[2]

The functional form of the Bellman equation has to be found providing an initial guess, and substituting it in the equation. If we posit that the solution $X(V) = AV^\beta$ and substitute it in the Bellman equation:

$$AV^\beta \left(\frac{1}{2}\sigma_v^2 \beta(\beta - 1) + \alpha_v \beta - \rho \right) = 0 \qquad (5.18)$$

If β is a root of $\frac{1}{2}\sigma_v^2 \beta(\beta - 1) + \alpha\beta - \rho$, our initial guess satisfies the equation.

Since the Bellman equation is a linear second order homogeneous differential equation, the general solution can be represented as a linear combination of any two independent solutions. Hence, the general solution for the Bellman equation reads

$$X(V) = A_1 V^{\beta_1} + A_2 V^{\beta_2} \qquad (5.19)$$

The solutions for β_1 and β_2 are

$$\beta_1 = \frac{1}{2} - \alpha_v/\sigma_v^2 + \sqrt{[\alpha_v/\sigma_v^2 - 1/2]^2 + 2\rho/\sigma_v^2} \qquad (5.20)$$

$$\beta_2 = \frac{1}{2} - \alpha_v/\sigma_v^2 - \sqrt{[\alpha_v/\sigma_v^2 - 1/2]^2 + 2\rho/\sigma_v^2} \qquad (5.21)$$

Taking into account that $\alpha_v < \rho$ it is easy to see that $\beta_1 > 1$ and $\beta_2 < 0$. The final step consists of finding the constants A_1 and A_2 and the threshold value at which the firm should invest V^*. This can be done by using the boundary conditions. Equation (5.15) implies that $A_2 = 0$, so that the solution becomes:

$$X(V) = A_1 V^{\beta_1} \tag{5.22}$$

Using Equations (5.16) and (5.17) it can now be derived that

$$A_1 V^{*\beta_1} = V^* - I \tag{5.23}$$

and

$$\beta_1 A_1 V^{*\beta_1 - 1} = 1 \tag{5.24}$$

This gives:

$$V^* = \frac{\beta_1}{\beta_1 - 1} I \tag{5.25}$$

and

$$A = \frac{(\beta_1 - 1)^{\beta_1 - 1}}{\beta_1^{\beta_1} I^{\beta_1 - 1}} \tag{5.26}$$

Since $\beta_1 > 1$, Equation (5.25) shows that $V^* > I$, which is the most important result of this model. It shows that due to irreversibility and uncertainty the critical value to invest is larger than the sunk costs, which is another way of expressing that the *naive NPV* rule does not hold anymore. In other words, if $V > I$ and $V < V^*$, the firm does not invest. There is a range of inaction which does not exist in the neoclassical model. According to the orthodox neoclassical model a firm should invest when $V > I$ or when $q > 1$, where $q = V/I$. The new approach emphasizes the importance of considering the *killing* of the option to invest when a firm decides to invest. This means that when a firm invests firm value raises by $V - X(V)$ rather than by V. Hence, the new decision rule becomes: invest if $V - X(V) > I$ or if $V > I + X(V)$. This implies that q should be defined to be net of the option value. Thus, the correct q is equal to $(V - X(V))/I$, so that again the threshold q^* that justifies investment is 1. This way of measuring marginal q is called the *net of the option value* concept of q by Dixit and Pindyck. However, since q is usually measured in the conventional way as V/I, the threshold q^* for investment is $\frac{\beta_1}{\beta_1 - 1} > 1$. Hence, due to irreversibility and delay there is a range of inaction for values of $q > 1$ and $q < q^*$. Note that Dixit and Pindyck call the conventional way of measuring q the *value of assets in place* concept of q since it is calculated once the investment is completed, ignoring the negative effect of killing the option when the next project is undertaken.

The final question concerns the magnitude of the wedge between the traditional net present value investment criterion and the new view. Several authors have shown that the wedge can become quite large for reasonable parameter values. Moreover, by totally differentiating the quadratic expression for β and by evaluating this expression at β_1 it can be shown that $\frac{d\beta_1}{d\sigma} < 0$ so that $\frac{\beta_1}{\beta_1 - 1}$ increases and the wedge is larger, the greater the amount of uncertainty. Hence, the McDonald and Siegel model provides another reason why uncertainty may lead to a decline in investment: it increases the wedge which may lead to a delay in investment. This implies that it is extremely important to consider the interaction between irreversibility and uncertainty when an investment rule is derived.

5.4   OPTIMAL IRREVERSIBLE INVESTMENT

The McDonald and Siegel model deals with the optimal timing of an investment project. The model does not derive a proper dynamic investment function. In a number of recent papers dynamic investment models are derived in which the implications of irreversibility and the possibility to delay are taken into account. The model of Bertola (1998) is a well known example in this category.

The Bertola model considers a firm with a Cobb-Douglas production function:

$$Q = (K_t^\alpha (A_t L_t)^{1-\alpha})^\phi \qquad (5.27)$$

where Q is production, K the capital stock, L employment, and ϕ indicates the return to scale in production. Constant returns to scale implies $\phi = 1$. In line with the Holthausen model (see Chapter 4), it is assumed that labour is completely variable and can therefore always be determined after all variables have become certain. Capital is quasi fixed. The price p is given by the following constant elasticity demand function (an isoelastic demand curve):

$$p = D_t Q_t^{\mu-1} \qquad (5.28)$$

where μ denotes the monopoly power of the firm, and D demand. For a competitive firm μ is 1. Bertola assumes $0 < \mu\phi < 1$. Hence, if there is a constant or increasing returns to scale production function ($\phi \geq 1$), the firm is imperfectly competitive ($\mu < 1$). If the firm is perfectly competitive the production function displays decreasing returns to scale. A situation in which the production function is constant returns to scale and the firm is perfectly competitive, is precluded. In the next section it will be shown that this assumption has important implications. D determines the position of the demand function: it represent a demand shock.

Given the capital stock, the operating profit (Ψ) function of the firm, *i.e.* revenue minus the cost of the variable factors of production, is given by:

$$\Psi(K_t, w_t, D_t, A_t) = \max_{L_t}(p_t Q_t - w_t L_t) \tag{5.29}$$

The optimal choice of L_t maximizes the operating profit. In the reduced form operating profits can now be derived to be[3]

$$\Psi(K_t, Z_t) = \frac{1}{1+\beta} K_t^{1+\beta} Z_t \tag{5.30}$$

where:[4]

$$\beta = \frac{\phi\mu - 1}{1 - (1 - \alpha)\phi\mu}, -1 < \beta < 0 \tag{5.31}$$

and $Z_t = f(w_t, D_t, A_t; \alpha, \mu, \phi)$. Z summarizes the business conditions of the firm and depends positively on D and A and negatively on w.[5]

Uncertainty enters the model when it is assumed that A_t, D_t and w_t are stochastic and follow geometric Brownian motion stochastic processes. These stochastic processes imply that the business condition parameter Z follows a geometric Brownian motion with a constant mean growth of θ_z and variance σ_z^2:

$$dZ_t = Z_t \theta_z dt + Z_t \sigma_z dz_{zt} \tag{5.32}$$

where z is a Wiener process. The parameters in the stochastic process of Z are linear combinations of the corresponding parameters in the underlying processes of D, A and w. For reasons of convenience, Bertola solves his model by only considering Z, ignoring the underlying processes.

It is also assumed by Bertola that the purchase price of capital (p_k) follows a geometric Brownian motion:

$$dp_{k,t} = p_{k,t} \theta_p dt + p_{k,t} \sigma_p dz_{pt} \tag{5.33}$$

The firm is assumed to be risk neutral and it maximizes the expected discounted value of cash flows:

$$V(K_t, Z_t, p_{k,t}) = \max_{K_s} E_t \left[\int_t^\infty e^{-\rho(s-t)} \left(\Psi(K_s, Z_s) ds - p_{k,s} I_s \right) \right] \tag{5.34}$$

subject to:

$$dK_s = -\delta K_s ds + I_s \tag{5.35}$$

and the irreversibility constraint:

$$I_s \geq 0 \tag{5.36}$$

Bertola proves that the optimal irreversible investment policy implies that for all periods t the following conditions hold:

$$E_t \left[\int_t^\infty e^{-(\rho+\delta)(s-t)} \frac{\partial \Psi(K_s, Z_s)}{\partial K_s} ds \right] = p_{k,t}; I_t > 0 \tag{5.37}$$

$$E_t \left[\int_t^\infty e^{-(\rho+\delta)(s-t)} \frac{\partial \Psi(K_s, Z_s)}{\partial K_s} ds \right] \leq p_{k,t}; I_t = 0 \tag{5.38}$$

Equation (5.37) can be explained as follows If the firm invests and there are no adjustment costs, the optimal policy requires that the *expected* present value of the gross return on the marginal unit of capital equals to the purchase price of one unit of capital. The condition is similar to Equation (4.38), recognizing that the Bertola model ignores adjustment costs. The left hand side of equation (5.37) denotes the present value at time t of additional revenue for the firm resulting from purchasing an extra unit of capital stock at time t. Again, it has be taken into account that income in periods $s > t$ from capital purchased in period t have to be discounted in order to express it in terms of period t units. Similarly the capital stock in period $s > t$ should be corrected by a depreciation factor. The left hand side of the equation is the shadow price of capital. The term on the right hand side denotes the cost of purchasing one unit of capital. Equation (5.38) simply states that a firm does not invest when the expected present value of the return on the marginal unit of capital is less than the purchase price of capital.

The problem is to find an investment rule that satisfies the above conditions. Bertola shows that the optimal investment policy implies that the firm invests when:

$$\frac{1}{r + \delta + \delta\beta - \theta_z} \frac{\partial \Psi(K_t, Z_t)}{\partial K_t} = p_{k,t} c \tag{5.39}$$

where $c = \frac{\rho}{\rho-1}$; $\rho = f(\sigma^2, \delta, \theta_p, \theta_z, \beta)$ and $\sigma^2 = h(\sigma_z^2, \sigma_p^2)$. Bertola shows that $\rho > \frac{-1}{\beta}$. Since $-1 < \beta < 0$, this implies that $\rho > 1$ and therefore $c > 1$. Since $\frac{\partial \Psi(K_t, Z_t)}{\partial K_t} = K_t^\beta Z_t$ this condition can be rewritten as:

$$\frac{K_t^\beta Z_t}{r + \delta + \delta\beta - \theta_z} = p_{k,t} c \tag{5.40}$$

The left hand side of Equation (5.40) is equal to the discounted marginal revenue of capital installed at time t, regardless of the possibility of installing more capital in the future. The equation shows that the firm only undertakes an irreversible investment when the expected revenue product of investment exceeds the cost of investment by the factor c. The optimal investment rule determining the desired stock of capital K^* is given by:

$$K_t^*(Z_t, p_{k,t}) = \left(c \frac{(r + \delta + \delta\beta - \theta_z)p_{k,t}}{Z_t} \right)^{1/\beta} \qquad (5.41)$$

K_t^* increases when Z_t increases or $p_{k,t}$ or c decreases since $\beta < 0$. Bertola shows that c increases with σ. Hence, an increase in uncertainty makes the firm more reluctant to invest and the desired capital stock decreases. In other words, an increase in the variability of the firm's environment increases the investment trigger. This again gives rise to the *bad news principle* of irreversible investment. Higher variability (increased uncertainty) does not symmetrically affect outcomes in the bad and the good states. For instance, if demand is unexpectedly low (bad state), the firm cannot undo the decision. However, if demand is unexpectedly high (good state), the firm can easily increase capital stock. Hence, the irreversibility constraint only applies in case of bad news. This implies that only potential bad news affects the current investment decision; potential good news has no effect at all. Higher uncertainty implies that the bad news case is more likely to occur. The firm hedges against bad news by adjusting the desired capital stock downwards. The optimal investment policy is that whenever $K < K^*$ the firm adjusts the capital stock immediately. If $K < K^*$, the firm does not invest and lets the capital stock be reduced by depreciation. Bertola also reformulates his model in line with an optimal timing approach (see Section 5.2). The proof is left to the reader.

5.5   PERFECT COMPETITION AND CONSTANT RETURNS TO SCALE

In contrast to the models of Hartman and Abel (see Chapter 4), Bertola's model ignores the case of a perfect competitive firm with a constant returns to scale production function. Caballero (1991) shows that the effect of an increase in uncertainty on investment depends on the assumption with respect to returns to scale and competition. He shows that an increase in uncertainty always has a positive effect on investment for a perfectly competitive firm with a constant returns to scale production function, even in the case where investment is irreversible.[6] An increase in uncertainty only has a negative effect on investment when the firm is either not perfectly competitive or has a decreasing return to scale production function in addition to the irreversibility of investment. The main reason for this outcome is that under constant returns to scale and perfect competition the reduced form profit function is a linear function of the capital stock; hence, the marginal revenue product of capital does not depend on the capital stock. In that case the firm is indifferent with respect to the level of the capital stock either now or in the future. This implies that the irreversibility of investment does not affect the optimal investment decision. Another way of stating the above is that under perfect competition and constant returns to scale there are no intertemporal links in the sense that investment now does not depend on the capital stock of tomorrow or yesterday.

Caballero uses a simple two period model to show that under perfect competition and constant returns to scale an increase in uncertainty, for a risk neutral firm always has a positive effect on investment. Under perfect competition the demand function reads:

$$p_t = Z_t \tag{5.42}$$

where Z_t is a lognormal random walk process: $Z_t = Z_{t-1}e^{\varepsilon_t}$ and where ε_t is normally distributed with mean $-\sigma^2/2$ and a variance σ^2. p_t is the price level. The production function is a constant returns to scale Cobb-Douglas function:

$$Q = AL^\alpha K^{1-\alpha} \tag{5.43}$$

Following the approach set out in the previous section, it is easy to show that the reduced form equation for operating profits depends linearly on capital stock and is given by:

$$\Psi = hZ_t^n K_t \tag{5.44}$$

where $h = (1-\alpha)A^{1/(1-\alpha)}\left(\frac{\alpha}{w}\right)^{\alpha/(1-\alpha)}$ and $n = \frac{1}{1-\alpha} > 1$. Caballero uses the following cost function (see Section 4.3):

$$C(I) = I + [I > 0]\gamma_1 I^\beta + [I < 0]\gamma_2 |I|^\beta \tag{5.45}$$

Ignoring from discounting and depreciation, the firm faces the following optimization problem:

$$V_1(K_0, Z_1) = \max_{I_1} \Psi(K_1, Z_1) - C(I_1) + E_1[V_2(K_1, Z_2] \tag{5.46}$$

subject to $K_1 = K_0 + I_1$. V_i denotes the value function at time i. The first order condition reads:

$$\Psi_{K_1}(K_0 + I_1, Z_1) - C_I(I_1) + E_1[V_{2K_1}(K_0 + I_1, Z_2)] = 0 \tag{5.47}$$

with the terminal value function:

$$V_2(K_1, Z_2) = \max_{I_2} \Psi(K_1 + I_2, Z_2) - C(I_2) \tag{5.48}$$

Maximizing the value function in the second period yields:

$$hZ_2^n - I[I_2 > 0](1 + \gamma_1 \beta I_2^{\beta-1}) - [I_2 < 0]\left(1 - \gamma_2 \beta |I_2|^{\beta-1}\right) \tag{5.49}$$

There are two cases for I_2, one in which $I_2 > 0$ or $hZ_2^n \geq 1$:

$$I_2 = \left[\frac{hZ_2^n - 1}{\gamma_1 \beta}\right]^{1/(\beta-1)} \tag{5.50}$$

and the other case in which $I_2 < 0$ or $hZ_2^n < 1$:

$$I_2 = -\left[\frac{1 - hZ_2^n}{\gamma_2 \beta}\right]^{1/(\beta-1)} \tag{5.51}$$

Hence, investment in period 2 does not depend on the capital stock in the previous period. The marginal revenue product of capital V_{2,K_1} equals $\Psi_{K_1}(K_1 + I_2, Z_2)$. Using Equation (5.44) it follows immediately that $V_{2,K_1} = hZ_t^n$. Since the marginal revenue product does not depend on K, the value function at time 2 is linearly dependent on K. The argument can be repeated for period 1. By using Equation (5.47) and the cost function, and by noting that $V_{2,K_1} = \Psi_K(K_1, Z_1) = hZ_t^n$; $\Psi_{K_1} = hZ_1^n$ the first order condition for period 1 reads:

$$hZ_1^n - [I_1 > 0](1 + \gamma_1 \beta I_1^{\beta-1}) - [I_1 < 0](1 - \gamma_2 \beta |I_1|^{\beta-1}) - E_1[h(Z_1 e^{\varepsilon_2})^n] \tag{5.52}$$

Applying Ito's lemma we can show that:

$$E_1 e^{\varepsilon_2 n} = \frac{\sigma^2}{2}(n(n-1)) \tag{5.53}$$

Therefore, for $I_1 > 0$ or $hZ_1^n(1 + e^{(n(n-1)/2)\sigma^2}) \geq 1$:

$$I_1 = \left[\frac{hZ_1^n(1 + e^{(n(n-1)/2)\sigma^2} - 1)}{\gamma_1 \beta}\right]^{1/(\beta-1)} \tag{5.54}$$

and for $I_1 < 0$ or $hZ_1^n(1 + e^{(n(n-1)/2)\sigma^2}) < 1$:

$$I_1 = -\left[\frac{1 - hZ_1^n(1 + e^{(n(n-1)/2)\sigma^2})}{\gamma_2\beta}\right]^{1/(\beta-1)} \tag{5.55}$$

The important conclusion is that investment does not depend on past or future capital stocks. Caballero shows that this lack of intertemporal links also holds for the n period case. The outcome implies that the adjustment cost parameters are irrelevant to the effect of an increase in uncertainty on investment. This impact of uncertainty on investment depends on the numerator which does not include the adjustment cost parameters. Since $n > 1$ and $\beta \geq 1$, an increase in uncertainty raises investment or reduces disinvestment in line with the models by Hartman and Abel. The traditional irreversible investment case corresponds to $\gamma_1 = 0; \gamma_2 = \infty$ and $\beta = 1$. However, with perfect competition and constant returns to scale the size of the firm is indeterminate without convex adjustment costs. Therefore, to solve the model some convexity is needed ($\gamma_1 > 0$ and $\beta > 1$). The case of irreversible investment can be proxied by assuming that γ_1 is slightly above 0, β slightly above 1, and $\gamma_2 = \infty$. Still, the model shows that an increase in uncertainty has a positive effect on investment. Hence, for a perfectly competitive risk neutral firm with a constant returns to scale production function, an increase in uncertainty always has a positive effect on investment.

Caballero shows that imperfect competition or a decreasing returns to scale production function is required to obtain negative effects from an increase in uncertainty on investment. If competition is imperfect or the production function has decreasing returns to scale, the marginal profitability of capital depends on the capital stock. It may then be the case that investment now results in too high or too low levels of capital tomorrow, vis- à-vis the desired capital stock. If adjustment costs are asymmetric in the sense that the costs of decreasing the capital stock exceed the cost of increasing the capital stock, or if the costs of decreasing the capital stock become infinite (irreversibility), too much capital is worse than too little capital. In such a case, an increase in uncertainty may have a negative effect on investment.

5.6 LIMITED REVERSIBILITY AND EXPANDABILITY

Both the McDonald and Siegel (1986) model and the Bertola (1998) model rely on the extreme assumption of complete irreversibility of investment. On the other hand, the basic neoclassical Jorgensen model assumes costless reversibility. Obviously, reality will be somewhere in between. Therefore, recent papers have tried to model partial irreversibility resulting from a difference between the price at which the firm can purchase capital and the price at which it can sell capital. In terms of the adjustment cost function, these papers use a piecewise linear adjustment cost specification (see Section 4.3). Well known examples are Abel and Eberly (1994,1996) and Abel *et al.* (1996). These models explore the options associated with the partial reversibility assumption. The Abel and Eberly (1994) model also assumes partial reversibility but they do not explain the option characteristics of their model.

This section explains the model by Abel, Dixit, Eberly and Pindyck, which will be referred to as the ADEP model. There are two main differences between the ADEP model and the basic irreversibility models. First, by assuming a constant purchase price of capital, the opportunity cost of waiting considered by most of the irreversibility literature consists only of foregone profits. In the ADEP model the purchase price of capital may increase over time, which implies an additional opportunity cost of waiting. The ability to expand is costly, so that the model allows for *limited* expandability. Second, in contrast with most of the irreversibility literature, the ADEP model allows for disinvestment. However, the resale price of capital may be less than the current purchase price, so that reversibility becomes costly. Hence, the model allows for *limited* reversibility. In the extreme case where the resale price is zero, investment is *de facto* irreversible. The ADEP model shows that in a world with uncertain future returns, costly expandability and reversibility imply two options. The possibility to resell capital creates a put option, whereas the possibility to delay, and thus future expandability creates a call option. The implication is that the marginal valuation of capital consists of the sum of the expected present value of capital when the firm is not allowed to sell or purchase any capital and the effects of the put option to sell and the call option to purchase capital. An increase in uncertainty will then negatively affect investment through an increase in the value of the call option but will positively affect investment by means of an increase in the value of the put option.

The ADEP model is a simple two period model in which a firm optimizes the expected present value of period 1 and period 2 cash flows by setting an optimal value for the period 1 capital stock. In the first period the firm purchases capital K_1 at a cost b. The first period total returns are given by $r(K_1)$. In the second period returns are uncertain and they are given by $R(K,e)$, where e is stochastic, distributed according to a known probability density $f(e)$. It is assumed that the marginal product of capital $(R_K(K,e))$ is nonnegative and strictly decreases in K and increases in e.

The model defines two critical values of e:

$$R_K(K_1, e_L) = b_L \qquad (5.56)$$

$$R_K(K_1, e_H) = b_H \qquad (5.57)$$

where b_L and b_H are the resale and purchase price of capital in the second period, respectively. It is assumed that $b_L \leq b_H$. $R_K(K_1, e)$ is the period 2 marginal return to period 1 installed capital. There is costly reversibility in case $b_L < b$ and costly expandability when $b_H > b$.

In the second period, when e is known, capital stock will be adjusted to a new optimal level $K_2(e)$. If $e > e_H$ the period 2 marginal return to period 1 installed capital exceeds the purchase price of capital; a firm can then make profits to buy new capital. It is most profitable to buy capital until the marginal return of capital equals the purchase price; therefore the period 2 optimal level of capital is determined by:

$$R_K(K_2(e), e) = b_H \qquad (5.58)$$

On the other hand, in the case where $e < e_L$ it is optimal to sell capital. The period 2 optimal level of capital is then given by:

$$R_K(K_2(e), e) = b_L \qquad (5.59)$$

Finally, if $e_L \leq e \leq e_H$, the firm should neither purchase nor sell capital, so that:

$$K_2(e) = K_1 \qquad (5.60)$$

The traditional Jorgensen model in which investment is completely and costlessly reversible and expandable, corresponds with a situation where the wedge between the purchase and sale price of capital is zero, and therefore $b_L = b = b_H$. This implies an optimal investment rule which ensures that capital will be purchased or sold, so that the marginal revenue product will never deviate from its user cost. The case of irreversible investment corresponds to a value of $b_L = 0$. This implies that a firm is never able to sell capital and hence that the optimal investment policy is characterized by a so-called one trigger policy. The purchase of capital guarantees that the marginal value of capital never exceeds the trigger given by b_H. If the marginal product of capital happens to be below the trigger, the firm's optimal investment is zero, and hence there is a range of inaction. In case of costly reversibility the optimal investment policy is a two trigger policy. The firm prevents the marginal revenue product from rising above the upper trigger value by purchasing capital, whereas it prevents the marginal revenue product from falling below the lower trigger value by selling capital. The range of inaction is given by the values of the marginal revenue product between the two trigger values. [7]

The value of a firm with K_1 capital stock in period 1 $V(K_1)$, equals the expected present value of cash flows. It consists of period 1 total returns plus the discounted value of period 2 returns. The (expected value) of the period 2 returns depend on the value of e; thus:

$$V(K_1) = r(K_1) + \gamma \int_{-\infty}^{e_L} (R(K_2(e), e) + b_L [K_1 - K_2(e)]) dF(e)$$

$$+ \gamma \int_{e_L}^{e_H} R(K_1, e) dF(e)$$

$$+ \gamma \int_{e_H}^{\infty} (R(K_2(e), e) - b_H [K_2(e) - K_1]) dF(e) \qquad (5.61)$$

where γ is a constant discount factor, $F(e)$ is the cumulative distribution function; and $[K_1 - K_2(e)]$ and $[K_2(e) - K_1]$ determine the amount of capital sold and purchased, respectively. The above equation can be rewritten as:

$$V(K_1) = G(K_1) + \gamma P(K_1) - \gamma C(K_1) \qquad (5.62)$$

where:

$$G(K_1) = r(K_1) + \gamma \int_{-\infty}^{\infty} R(K_1, e) dF(e) \qquad (5.63)$$

$$P(K_1) = \int_{-\infty}^{e_L} ([R(K_2(e), e) - b_L K_2(e)] - [R(K_1, e) - b_L K_1]) dF(e) \qquad (5.64)$$

$$F(K_1) = \int_{e_H}^{\infty} (-[R(K_2(e), e) - b_H K_2(e)] + [R(K_1, e) - b_H K_1]) dF(e) \qquad (5.65)$$

$G(K_1)$ represents the expected present value of total returns in period 1 and 2 when it is not allowed to sell or purchase capital, *i.e.* when the capital stock is constant. $P(K_1)$ is the value of the put option, *i.e.* the value of the option to sell capital in period 2 against a price of b_L. $F(K_1)$ is the value of the call option, *i.e.* the value of the possibility to purchase capital in period 2 at a price of b_H.

The decision problem of the firm reads:

$$\max_{K_1} V(K_1) - bK_1 \qquad (5.66)$$

The first order condition is:[8]

$$V'(K_1) = N(K_1) + \gamma P'(K_1) - \gamma F'(K_1) = b \qquad (5.67)$$

where:

$$N(K_1) \;=\; r'(K_1) + \gamma \int_{-\infty}^{\infty} R_K(K_1, e) dF(e) > 0 \tag{5.68}$$

$$P'(K_1) \;=\; \int_{-\infty}^{e_L} [b_L - R_K(K_1, e)] \, dF(e) \geq 0 \tag{5.69}$$

$$F'(K_1) \;=\; \int_{e_H}^{\infty} [R_K(K_1, e) - b_H] \, dF(e) \geq 0 \tag{5.70}$$

Equation (5.67) shows that the marginal valuation of capital, the shadow value of capital, consists of three parts. The first part ($N(K_1)$) represents the marginal return for period 1 and 2 when the firm is not allowed to sell or to purchase capital. The second part ($P'(K_1)$) gives the effect of the option to sell capital, *i.e.* the marginal put option; the opportunity to reduce the capital stock increases the expected marginal revenue product of capital. The third term ($F'(K_1)$) represents the effect of the opportunity to purchase capital, the effect of the marginal call option. The possibility to increase the capital stock in the future has a negative effect on the marginal revenue product of capital. The reason for this is that by calculating the marginal revenue product of capital relevant for the investment decision, we consider the effect of investing in the *next* project. However, by investing in the next project, the option to invest is killed and hence its value should be subtracted in order to arrive at the true marginal revenue product of capital.[9]

The above condition is the correct marginality condition. However, in reality it is very difficult to account for the fact that in the case where the capital stock in future periods change, the marginal return will also change along the optimal path. Therefore, in reality the net present value is often calculated by ignoring the possibility of purchasing or selling capital. This implies that managers usually calculate the NPV as:

$$N(K_1) = r'(K_1) + \gamma \int_{-\infty}^{\infty} R_K(K_1, e) dF(e) \tag{5.71}$$

The investment rule based on this calculation is called the naive NPV rule: a firm should invest whenever the marginal revenue product, as given by $N(K_1)$, exceeds the purchase price of capital b. However, by using Equation (5.67) it can be shown that the correct investment rule is:

$$N(K_1) = b - \gamma P'(K_1) + \gamma F'(K_1) \tag{5.72}$$

Hence, a firm that calculates the NPV naively, should adjust the cost of capital by taking into account the negative effect of the call option and the positive

effect of the put option.[10] Only in the case where the naive NPV exceeds
the adjusted cost of capital, should the firm invest immediately. Note that in
a model with complete irreversibility the put option does not exist, and thus
only the effect of the call option should be taken into account.
The option value multiple ϕ is defined by:

$$\phi = \frac{N(K_1)}{b} = 1 + \gamma \left[F'(K_1) - P'(K_1) \right] \tag{5.73}$$

The option value multiple determines to what extend the naive NPV exceeds
the investment cost. In the case where capital is completely irreversible and
unexpandable, $b_L = 0$ and $b_H = \infty$. This implies that $F'(K_1) = P'(K_1) = 0$ since
the firm cannot sell nor purchase capital in the next period. When investment is
completely irreversible but partly expandable, the call option has some value;
in this case the option value multiple is greater than 1. This is the effect
usually emphasized in the irreversibility literature. It clearly shows that not
only irreversibility but also expandability is important. In fact, expandability
corresponds to the above mentioned importance of the possibility to delay. The
possibility to delay (expandability) generates a call option. On the other hand, if
investment is partly reversible the put option becomes valuable. Now the option
value multiple may even fall below 1, which will be the case when capital is
completely unexpandable.

What is the effect of an increase in uncertainty on the marginal valuation
of capital and thus on investment in this general model of partial reversibility
and partial expandability? Abel *et al.* show that there are three effects. First,
in line with the orthodox models an increase in uncertainty increases the naive
NPV and hence investment in the case where $R(K_1, e)$ is a convex function of
e. Second, in line with the analyses of the irreversibility model an increase in
uncertainty increases the value of the marginal call option. This has a negative
effect on investment. Finally, an increase in uncertainty increases the value of
the marginal put option. This again has a positive effect on investment. Hence,
the net effect of an increase in uncertainty is unclear and depends on the degree
of irreversibility and expandability; the higher the degree of irreversibility and
expandability, the more likely an increase in uncertainty is to negatively affect
investment. On the other hand, in the case where capital stock becomes more
reversible but at the same time less expandable, the probability that an increase
in uncertainty has a positive effect on investment rises.

5.7 NON-LINEAR EFFECTS OF UNCERTAINTY

Most papers argue that the uncertainty-investment relationship is linear. However, some recent theoretical analyses suggest that the investment-uncertainty relationship is not monotonic and probably can be represented by an inverted U curve. For instance, Abel and Eberly (1999, p. 354) show that for low levels of uncertainty the capital stock increases with uncertainty, while high levels of uncertainty depress investment. This hump-shaped behaviour in their model results from a trade-off between a user costs effect and a hangover effect.

Kahneman and Tversky (1979) provide additional theoretical reasons for an inverted U-curve relation between investment and uncertainty. They argue that there is risk-seeking behaviour over the domain of small losses if the utility of an agent depends on gains or losses, instead of final income states. If investment behaviour were derived from such a nonlinear utility function, a firm would prefer to take some risk for a range of small losses, which are *e.g.* due to an increase in uncertainty. In this situation, the investment-uncertainty relationship would be positive up to a certain threshold, and negative thereafter.

Probably the best explanation for a non-linear relationship between investment and uncertainty is given by Sarkar (2000). The model is an adjusted version of the seminal McDonald and Siegel (1986) options pricing model. As explained before, McDonald and Siegel show that investment irreversibility and uncertainty drives a wedge between the value of the project and the investment costs. By deriving an exact expression of the wedge, they are able to show to what extent the standard net present value rule of investment has to be adjusted. The model assumes that the firm controls the timing of a totally irreversible investment problem and in each period therefore chooses between investing (stopping) or waiting (continuation) one more period. An increase in uncertainty lowers the trigger value of investment.

Sarkar points out that an increase in uncertainty also increases the probability that the investment threshold will be passed so that the probability that investment will take place within a specified time period increases. Since there is a positive and a negative effect, the overall effect of uncertainty on investment becomes ambiguous. By means of model simulations Sarkar shows that the additional positive "hitting" effect dominates the negative threshold effect for low levels of uncertainty.

5.8 CONCLUSIONS

This chapter reviews the recent theoretical literature on models for investment under uncertainty. The aim of this chapter and the previous one is to examine the effect of an increase in uncertainty on the behaviour of the firm in general and on investment in particular. It is shown that the analysis of models which assume irreversibility is comparable to the types of analysis used in option theory. These models are therefore sometimes called the option approach to investment.

The effect of uncertainty on investment depends for example on the risk behaviour of the firm, the firm's mode of behaviour (perfect competition, or imperfect competition), the production technology, and the cost function. If the firm is risk averse, it is obvious that an increase in uncertainty may have a negative effect on investment. However, most investment under uncertainty models assume that firms are risk neutral.

In addition to risk neutrality, many authors assume that firms are perfectly competitive and produce with a constant returns to scale production function. In such a case, an increase in uncertainty always has a positive effect on investment, independent of the specification of the cost function. The reason is that these assumptions imply a marginal revenue product of capital which does not depend on the capital stock and which is a convex function of the variable which makes investment behaviour stochastic. Jensen's inequality then shows that an increase in uncertainty raises investment.

If we ignore the special case of a perfectly competitive firm with a constant returns to scale production function, an increase in uncertainty may have a negative effect on investment by a risk neutral firm. This may be the case when adjustment costs are asymmetric in the sense that the costs of decreasing the capital stock exceed the cost of increasing the capital stock. An extreme example is that of irreversible investment, which implies that the adjustment costs of decreasing the capital stock are infinite. If this is the case, an increase in uncertainty probably affects investment negatively via a positive effect on the option value to wait. An increase in uncertainty raises the option value and hence leads to a delay in investment. In the case where investment is only partially irreversible and there is a possibility to sell the capital stock, the effect of an increase in uncertainty becomes ambiguous. An increase in uncertainty raises both the option value to wait and the option value to sell, with conflicting effects on investment.

Due to limited space we will not discuss all the contributions in the investment under uncertainty literature. However, before ending this chapter it is relevant to mention one other issue: the long-run effect of uncertainty on investment. It may well be the case that due to irreversibility an increase in uncertainty has a negative effect on investment but that the long-run effect is positive. The reason is that irreversibility prevents the firm from reducing the capital stock. In that case there may be a *hang over effect* which leads to a long-run capital stock that exceeds the desired level (Abel and Eberly, 1999).

The surveys presented in Chapters 4 and 5 clearly show that the effect of an increase in uncertainty on investment is theoretically unclear. This implies that there is a need for empirical studies in order to gain a better picture of the investment-uncertainty relationship; therefore, the Chapter 6 deals with empirical studies on this relationship.

NOTES

1. It can be shown that even under certainty the option is valuable.
2. The third condition is necessary because of the existence of a *free boundary*. The first boundary is given by $V = 0$. However, the second boundary V^* must be determined as part of the solution.
3. This specification of reduced form operating profits is fairly standard. It is for example also used by Abel and Eberly (1996).
4. β determines the concavity of the profit function with respect to K. For a perfectly competitive firm with a constant return to scale production function β would be equal to 0 and hence the reduced form profit function would be a linear function of the capital stock (see also the next subsection). However, this situation is precluded by assumption since the value maximization problem is ill-defined for $\beta = 0$.
5. The exact value of Z is

$$Z = (1+\beta)\frac{\alpha\phi\mu}{\chi}((\phi u(1-\alpha))^{\frac{\phi\mu}{\chi}} - (\phi\mu(1-\alpha))^{\frac{1}{\chi}} D_t^{\frac{1}{\chi}} (\frac{w_t}{A_t})^{\frac{-\phi}{\chi}} \qquad (5.74)$$

   where $\chi = 1 - (1-\alpha)\phi\mu$ and $\varphi = (1-\alpha)\phi\mu$.
6. Pindyck (1993) shows that this result no longer holds when an industry equilibrium is considered and the effect of aggregate instead of idiosyncratic risk is examined.
7. The Abel and Eberly (1994, 1996) models also imply a two trigger policy.
8. If the purchase costs are ignored, $V'(K_1)$ by definition equals the value of marginal q. This correct measurement of marginal q accounts for the effects of the two options and therefore corresponds with the *net of option value* concept of marginal q.
9. The existence of both a put and a call option is a direct consequence of the assumption of partial reversibility and expandability. See Abel and Eberly (1996) for a similar result.
10. In an alternative explanation, Abel *et al.* (1996) show that the correct measurement of the marginal revenue product of capital equals the sum of the current period marginal return to capital plus the expected present value of the second period marginal return, where the second period marginal return is evaluated at the optimal level of capital in that period. In the naive way of calculating the marginal return of capital, the marginal return of capital in the second period is evaluated at the optimal level of capital in the first period.

6. Empirics of the Investment Uncertainty-Relationship*

6.1 INTRODUCTION

This chapter presents a survey of the empirical studies on the investment-uncertainty relationship. The investment decision is usually taken under genuine uncertainty. The investor needs to analyse future prospects of the investment project. Depending on the investor's attitude towards risk and the forecasts of future relevant variables, a stop/wait/go decision is taken. The most important characteristic of the investment decision is its dynamic nature. Economists are puzzled by the relationship between investment and uncertainty. As described in the previous chapters the traditional but counterintuitive opinion on the effect of uncertainty on investment, namely a positive relationship, is based on e.g. Hartman (1972) and Abel (1983). If the adjustment cost function is symmetric under conditions of perfect competition and constant returns to scale, the marginal product of capital is a convex function of uncertainty variables. Therefore, the higher the uncertainty, the higher the marginal productivity of capital will be. This encourages the firm to invest more.

The modern theory on the investment-uncertainty relationship emphasizes the role of irreversibility or costly reversibility of investment. Within the framework of irreversibility, investment opportunities are modelled as the firm holding call options on real assets. The firm has the right but not the obligation to buy the sequence of cash flows that is generated by the investment project in the future by paying certain investment costs. The key assumptions of the real option approach to investment behaviour are irreversibility and the possibility to delay the investment. The irreversibility property of investment implies that the firm cannot regret the outcome of the state once the investment decision has been made. If investment decisions are irreversible, investment will be more sensitive to the uncertainty faces the firm. Since the firm with more irreversible capital has a higher opportunity cost of capital (including the option value of investing right now), the firm will require a higher marginal

---

*This chapter is a revised version of Bo (1999a).

revenue product of capital to match the trigger for investment. By waiting the firm may gain more information. Consequently uncertainty directly affects the threshold that triggers the occurrence of investment, through which it affects the timing of investment and hence the scale of investment at a specific point in time (Bernanke, 1983, McDonald and Siegel, 1986, Pindyck 1991, Dixit and Pindyck 1994). Apparently, the real option approach to investment predicts a negative effect of uncertainty on investment.

There is a lively debate on the sign of the relationship between investment and uncertainty. As shown in Chapter 5, Caballero (1991) argues that the positive correlation between investment and uncertainty based on the Hartman-Abel prediction can be traced to the assumptions of perfect competition and constant returns to scale rather than the ignorance of irreversibility. He shows that even with the irreversibility assumption the positive uncertainty effect still holds as long as firms are perfectly competitive and at the same time have a constant returns production function. In other words, irreversibility does not necessarily lead to a negative investment-uncertainty relationship, as suggested by the real option approach to investment. Moreover, the real option approach to investment does not always predict the negative effects of uncertainty on investment. For example, Abel and Eberly (1999) demonstrate that the irreversibility property of investment may affect the investment-uncertainty relationship in a positive way due to the *hang over* effect in the long run. Moreover, in addition to the influence of irreversibility on the investment uncertainty relationship, other factors that may be important in for the determination of the sign of uncertainty effects, such as the risk attitude of the firm, the shape of the marginal productivity of capital, the degree of competition in product markets, and the substitutability of production factors, are often ignored. Hence, the sign of uncertainty effects on investment is ambiguous from a theoretical point of view.

This chapter addresses empirical tests of the uncertainty-investment relationship. The remainder of the chapter is structured as follows. Section 6.2 deals with measuring uncertainty. A survey of empirical studies on the investment-uncertainty relationship will be given in Section 6.3. Section 6.4 concludes this chapter.

6.2   MEASURING UNCERTAINTY

Theoretical models of investment under uncertainty assume that uncertainty can be modelled by a description of the stochastic process of the variables with which the firm is faced. These models implicitly assume that one is able to characterize all future outcomes by a probability distribution. This chapter follows this approach, although economists who disagree on this issue by arguing that investment decisions are taken under fundamental uncertainty (not knowing the distribution functions at all) should be acknowledged. In empirical work the specification of measurements that are derived from the theoretical probability functions need to be developed.

Theoretical models often assume that a variable p_t, of which future development is relevant to the investment decision can be modelled by a geometric Brownian motion:

$$dp_t = \mu_p p_t dt + \sigma_p p_t dz_p \qquad (6.1)$$

where μ_p represents the drift term, σ_p the volatility term, and z_p a Wiener process. Thus p_t is assumed to follow a continuous time random walk. The empirical problem is to determine the volatility parameter σ_p. As most of the data have a more discrete nature, most empirical models use a discrete approximation of σ_p.

One can use to estimate σ_p historical data, or *ex ante* survey approximations of volatility. Using historical data makes statistical inference possible. On the other hand, it is hard to mimic the special characteristics of volatility in this way. Using *ex ante* survey data perhaps makes this possible. Economic agents can simply be asked about their concerns about the future. The spread in the answers can be used to give an approximation of volatility. The subjective probability distributions assigned by agents are assumed to be consistent with the true probability distributions of random variables. This concept adheres more closely to the nature of volatility: it captures the intense ups and downs of the time series.

In the investment literature we can classify the methods used to measure uncertainty by:

1. the variance of the normal distribution of the variable itself (Bell and Campa, 1997, Ghosal, 1991, Pindyck 1986);
2. the variance of the unpredictable part of a stochastic process (Aizenman and Marion, 1993 and 1999, Bo, 1999b, Ghosal, 1995, Ghosal and Loungani, 1996, 2000, Leahy and Whited, 1996, and Peeters 1997);
3. the variance of geometric Brownian motion (Caballero and Pindyck, 1996, Pindyck and Solimano, 1993);
4. the General AutoRegressive Conditional Heteroskedastic model of volatility (Episcopos, 1995, Huizinga, 1993, Price 1995, 1996); and
5. the variance derived from survey data (Ferderer 1993a, 1993b, Guiso and Parigi, 1999, Pattillo 1998).

These methods will be discussed in more detail below. The first two methods will be lumped together, since it can be assumed that the unpredictable part of a stochastic process is simply given by the deviations from the mean.

6.2.1 The Variance of the Unpredictable Part of a Stochastic Process

The most popular approach to constructing an uncertainty measure is to derive the variance of the unpredictable part of a stochastic process. To do so, one first needs to select forecasting rules for the predictable part of the process. Once the process that governs the predictable part is known, we can compute the unpredictable part and its distribution. Using this probability function we can derive the volatility measure. More specifically, this method of measuring volatility can be summarized as follows:

1. set up a forecasting equation for the underlying uncertainty variable;

2. estimate the forecasting equation to obtain the unpredictable part of the fluctuations of that variable, *i.e.* the estimated residuals; and

3. compute the conditional standard deviations of the estimated residuals as the uncertainty measure of the concerned variable.

This method has been applied by Aizenman and Marion (1993, 1999), Ghosal (1995), Ghosal and Loungani (1996, 2000), and Peeters (1997). Issues of concern in the construction of the volatility measures involve the process that generates the predictable part of the stochastic process. Aizenman and Marion (1993) estimate the predictable part of a variable using a first order autoregressive process. They measure volatility by calculating the standard deviation of the differences between the actual and predicted series. In Ghosal and Loungani (1996) the forecasting equation of the predictable part of the relevant series (a price-index) is a second order autoregressive process with a time trend. The same forecasting rule is applied to predict firm's profits in Ghosal and Loungani (2000). Peeters (1997) models the process generating the underlying stochastic variable by an autoregressive process. She then divides the unpredictable part of the fluctuations of the random variable into a common shock term and an idiosyncratic shock. Next, she computes the standard deviations of the idiosyncratic shocks and weights the standard deviations by the firm's assets to equity ratio to finally obtain the measure of uncertainty.

As shown above, many different approximations of the predictable component of a stochastic process are found in the empirical literature. Once the Markov property of the series is assumed, any autoregressive forecasting equation can be used. It should be noted that the application of this method requires a stationary distribution of the unpredictable part of the stochastic process. To guarantee this, the observations and the predictable part of the process need to be co-integrated. Unfortunately, many empirical papers that apply this just take the stationarity of the distribution for granted. Several authors insert a trend term into the forecasting equation to deal with this problem (Ghosal and Loungani, 1996, 2000). The pretest of stationarity is expected to improve the precision of uncertainty measures. The unit root or cointegration test for instance can be applied for this purpose. Another problem in applying this method is that it is based on the assumption that either the unconditional variance of a random variable is constant or the conditional variance converges to a constant term, which in reality is not always the case.

6.2.2 The Variance Estimated from the Geometric Brownian Motion

Stochastic differential equations are used to model time-dependent volatility for continuous time observations. One popular model in this class is Brownian motion. Pindyck and Solimano (1993) and Caballero and Pindyck (1996) apply geometric Brownian motion to construct the conditional variance of the marginal productivity of capital (MR_k). These authors estimate the variance of the changes in MR_k from:

$$dMR_k = \bar{MR}_k dt + \sigma dz \qquad (6.2)$$

where dz is a standard Wiener process and $\bar{MR}_k$ is the mean of MR_k. σ is used as the measure of uncertainty to test the effect of uncertainty on investment.

Empirical applications of the geometric Brownian motion depend on the assumption of the process governing the volatility term σ, which can be assumed constant. If σ is assumed to vary, it may be either a known deterministic function of time or it may itself follow a Brownian motion. In the limited applications of the geometric Brownian motion in the field of investment, σ is assumed to be constant. There is, however, a major drawback to this method: the application of geometric Brownian motion requires continuous data. This makes the modelling of volatility using Brownian motion less popular than the GARCH-approach, which uses discrete time series data, and which will be discussed below.

6.2.3 The Generalized AutoRegressive Conditional Heteroskedasticity (GARCH)-Type Modelling of Volatility

The Generalized AutoRegressive Conditional Heteroskedasticity modelling of volatility offers an appealing measure of uncertainty in the sense that it allows for the time dependence of the second moment of random variables. In the previous two methods it is often assumed that volatility is simply constant. Using high-frequency financial data, simple statistical observation reveals that the shorter the period of the interval, the larger the probability of a fat tail of the distribution of the variable will be. Moreover, it is likely that the volatility of the variable displays clustering.

In the investment literature several studies apply the GARCH-type model to construct the conditional variance of random variables. Episcopos (1995) applies the AutoRegressive Conditional Heteroskedasticity (ARCH) model to U.S. data to estimate conditional variances for a number of interesting variables in order to test the impact of aggregate uncertainty on fixed investment using US data. Huizinga (1993) tests the impact of inflation uncertainty (and some other variables) on investment. His measure of uncertainty is the estimated conditional standard deviations of the underlying random variables from the ARCH model. Price (1996) investigates the long-run effect of uncertainty on investment in the UK manufacturing sector. The measure of uncertainty used is the conditional variance of manufacturing output estimated from a GARCH(1,1) model with the conditional mean specification of an autoregressive (AR(3)) process. Price (1995) tests the effect of aggregate uncertainty (the volatility of GDP) on manufacturing investment in the UK economy. The measure of uncertainty used is the conditional variance of GDP estimated from a GARCH-in-mean (GARCH-M) model.

The use of the GARCH approaches to model volatility seems to be attractive. However, the application of the GARCH model to measure volatility requires high frequency observations and longer time series. This may limit its applications in the field of investment. In addition, applying GARCH-type modelling requires the pretest for the existence of the ARCH effect of the conditional variance. Moreover, the common criticism of GARCH modelling is that the estimated conditional variance may be biased because of possible misspecification of the equation describing the conditional mean.

6.2.4 The Variance Derived from Survey Data

The main advantage of using survey data to construct uncertainty measures is that such data directly contain information on agents' expectations of future variables. Ferderer (1993a, 1993b), Guiso and Parigi (1999), and Pattillo (1998) employ survey data to derive uncertainty measures in their empirical investment studies. The uncertainty measure is simply proxied by taking either the standard deviation or the coefficient of variation of forecasted values for the variable of interest.

Ferderer (1993a) uses the risk premium embedded in the term structure of interest rates to measure uncertainty. The indicator of interest rate uncertainty is a linearization of the expected excess holding period return. He uses survey data technique to construct a measure of the market's expectation of the interest rate. By inserting expectations of the interest rate into the risk premium equation, he obtains measures of the volatility of the risk premium. Federer

(1993b) calculates standard deviations of the predicted values of each variable in each month. Next, he computes the average values of the standard deviations for each month. Finally, the uncertainty measure is defined as the ratio of the standard deviations to the average value of the standard deviations for each month.

Guiso and Parigi (1999) perform a cross-section analysis of the effect of demand uncertainty on investment using firm-level survey data for 549 Italian manufacturing firms in 1993. Pattillo (1998) investigates the impact of irreversibility on the investment uncertainty relationship. Her empirical analysis is based on survey data for a panel of Ghanaian manufacturing firms. The construction of the survey is similar in both papers: the managers of the firms were asked to assign subjective probabilities for given intervals of the percentage growth rate of the demand faced by the firm (one year and three years ahead). On the basis of the probability distributions assigned by the respondents, the expected mean growth and variance of demand are calculated. The variance is used as the measure of demand uncertainty.

The main advantage of using survey data to construct uncertainty measures is its forward-looking property. Therefore such uncertainty measures are able to represent individual perceptions of risks based on their own information set. However, this approach assumes that subjective probability distributions of events reflect objective probability distributions. In addition, it requires a large amount of respondents to obtain reliable uncertainty measures.

6.3   EMPIRICAL EVIDENCE ON THE
INVESTMENT-UNCERTAINTY RELATIONSHIP

Table 6.1 surveys emprical studies on the investment-uncertainty relationship. The table presents the method of measuring uncertainty, and variables used to measure uncertainty, variables which are believed to interact with these uncertainty measures. Empirical studies appear to strongly support the negative effect of uncertainty on investment: 18 out of 21 papers report a negative sign of uncertainty effect on investment.

Before dealing with the explanations for these outcomes, it is relevant to consider the degree to which uncertainty affects investment. There are large differences, depending on the source of uncertainty, the way uncertainty is quantified, the investment model and data used. For example, Guiso and Parigi (1999) find that an increase of 5 per cent in demand uncertainty decreases investment by 0.44 per cent. Pattillo (1998) finds that an increase of 5 per cent in demand uncertainty only decreases investment by 0.01 per cent. Leahy and Whited (1996) show that a 1 per cent increase in the variance leads to a 0.17 per cent fall in the rate of investment, whereas Pindyck (1986) argues that a 1 per cent increase in the variance of stock returns leads to a 3 percentage point drop in the growth rate of investment. In order to improve the precision of the tests for the effect of uncertainty, Pagan and Ullah (1988) propose to use instrumental variables of the constructed risk terms.

6.3.1 Irreversibility and the Investment-Uncertainty Relationship

In Table 6.1, 12 of the papers explain the negative effect by referring to the irreversibility hypothesis (Aizenman and Marion (1993, 1999), Bell and Campa (1997), Caballero and Pindyck (1996), Episcopos (1995), Ferderer (1993a, 1993b), Leahy and Whited (1996), Pattillo (1998), Pindyck (1986), Pindyck and Solimano (1993), and Price (1996)). Among these, Pattillo (1998), Caballero and Pindyck (1996) and Pindyck and Solimano (1993) directly test the effect of uncertainty on the threshold that triggers investment. Other papers test the irreversibility hypothesis in an indirect way by considering the investment-uncertainty relation for different groups of firms, or different investment projects that are supposed to have different degrees of irreversibility.

The indirect test of the impact of the degree of irreversibility on the investment-uncertainty relationship requires empirical proxies of irreversibility. Guiso and Parigi (1999) use two different indicators of irreversibility of installed capital:

1.   the degree of access to secondary markets for installed capital goods;

2.   the degree of cyclical volatility of the firm's industry.

The latter proxy is based on the assumption that a more cyclical industry implies that capital is more illiquid. They find a negative sign of demand uncertainty for all groups of firms. Moreover, the negative effects are greater for the groups of firms with more irreversible capital goods.

Pattillo (1998) uses the ratio of real sales value of the capital stock to its real replacement value as the indicator of the irreversibility of investment. She also finds evidence for the fact that the negative uncertainty effect is significantly greater for firms with irrversible investment. In her reduced form Tobit estimation, the estimated coefficient of demand uncertainty is significantly negative for the firms that have more irreversible capital, while the estimated coefficient of demand uncertainty is insignificant for the firms that have more reversible capital. Finally, Bell and Campa (1997) and Pindyck (1986) also provide evidence for a more probable negative uncertainty-investment relationship when the degree of irreversibility is higher.

Table 6.1   The sign of the investment-uncertainty relationship

AUTHOR(S)	SIGN[a]	UNCERTAINTY SOURCE	INTERACTION
NORMAL VARIANCE			
Bell and Campa (1997)	M	Exchange rate demand, output price	Irreversibility
Ghosal (1991)	N	Demand	Firm size
Pindyck (1986)	N	Stock returns	Irreversibility, firm size
UNPREDICTED PART			
Aizenman and Marion (1993, 1999)	N	Macroeconomic	
Bo (1999b)	N	Profit, interest rate	Financial constraints
Ghosal (1995)	P	Output price	
Ghosal and Loungani (1996)	N	Output price	Product competition
Ghosal and Loungani (2000)	N	Profit	Firm size
Peeters (1997)	N	Demand, output price investment price	Firm size, leverage
BROWNIAN MOTION			
Caballero and Pindyck (1996)	N	Industry, idiosyncratic	
Pindyck and Solamino (1993)	N	Capital productivity	
GARCH			
Episcopos (1995)	N	Multiple	
Huizinga (1993)	M	Inflation, wage, profit, price	
Price (1996)	N	Manufacturing output	
Price (1995)	N	GDP	
SURVEY DATA			
Ferderer (1993a)	N	Interest rates, inflation, unemployment	
Guiso and Parigi (1999)	N	Demand	Irreversibility, fin. constraints, product comp., substitutability
Pattillo (1998)	N	Demand	
VAR-MODEL			
Leahy and Whited (1996)	N	Stock market	Firm β, substitutability
RISK PREMIUM			
Ferderer (1993b)	N	Interest rate	

[a]Y represents a positive relationship, N a negative and M mixed evidence.

6.3.2   Capital Market Imperfections

Some empirical studies find evidence that the effect of uncertainty on investment provides information on the link between capital market imperfections
and investment. For instance, firms with high leverage are believed to have
a higher probability of financial distress, which implies that these firms will
react more strongly to a high degree of uncertainty and will perhaps be more
risk averse than firms with a normal leverage. Firm-level studies deal with this
issue by distinguishing between subgroups of firms on the basis of the level of
debt within the firm (see Peeters, 1997). In the empirical studies that have been
reviewed here, four papers made an attempt to test the link between the effect
of uncertainty on investment and capital market imperfections.

Peeters divides the sample on the basis of leverage. She estimates models for
Belgian and Spanish firms; using a Euler investment model for Belgian firms
she finds a slightly significant negative effect of sales uncertainty on investment
by both the low and high leverage firms. For Spanish firms she finds a negative
effect of price uncertainty only for low leverage firms. Her explanation is that
firms that rely more on internal finance (and have less debt) are apparently
more affected by uncertainty.

Ghosal and Loungani (1996) use firm size as a proxy for access to external
capital. Industries dominated by small firms are assumed to be more severely
constrained by capital market imperfections than large-firm-dominated industries. They find evidence that the impact of profit uncertainty is larger for small-
firm-dominated industries than that for large-firm-dominated industries. The
estimated uncertainty elasticity ranges from −0.344 to −0.881 in the former
and from −0.124 to −0.240 in the latter. Since they split the sample based
on the degree to which firms can exchange information with outside lenders,
their result again provides some evidence that there is an interaction between
the effect of uncertainty and capital market imperfections. The link between
uncertainty effects and financial constraints is also taken into account in the
investment model chosen by Ghosal and Loungani. They investigate the effect
of uncertainty within the framework of a liquidity constraint-type investment
equation.

Bo (1999b) uses a q model for a panel of Dutch firms. She finds evidence that
severe uncertainty effects are associated with more serious financial distress
faced by the firm. Profit uncertainty and interest rate volatility are found to be
more important for investment decisions taken by high-debt firms than those
decisions taken by low-debt firms.

Guiso and Parigi (1999) find that the value of estimated coefficient of the
demand uncertainty decreases in absolute value when an indicator of credit
market access is added to the investment equation. Although the estimated
coefficient becomes less significant in the presence of the credit rationing indi-

cator, the result indicates that financial constraints may lead to a more severe demand uncertainty effect on investment. Although the effect of capital market imperfections is not documented explicitly in Ghosal (1991) and Pindyck (1986), these studies do show that the negative effects of uncertainty on investment are smaller for larger firms. Since larger firms are usually firms that have less trouble in obtaining external capital, these studies strongly suggest that investment studies should consider the interaction between capital market imperfections and uncertainty simultaneously.

6.3.3   The Degree of Competition in Product Markets

The degree of competition in product markets also affects the investment-uncertainty relationship. Guiso and Parigi (1999) explicitly test the hypothesis that a change in the degree of competition in product markets leads to a change in the effect of demand uncertainty on investment. Using the profit margin on unit price as an indicator of market power, they divide the sample into high versus low market power groups. Their results show that the estimated coefficients of demand uncertainty for the firms with low market power are smaller in absolute value than for firms with high market power. This is the same as saying that a lower degree of competition in product markets is associated with a greater negative demand uncertainty effect on investment. Although this is in line with the theory of Hartman (1972), it may nevertheless seem somewhat surprising, since one would expect monopolists to have larger buffers and so to be less vulnerable to unexpected volatility.

Ghosal and Loungani (1996) find strong evidence that there is a big difference in the effect of price uncertainty on investment between more and less competitive industries. Their indicator of product market competition is the four-firm seller concentration ratio. They define industries with 20 per cent concentration over the entire sample period as more competitive industries and industries with 60 per cent as less competitive industries. They find no effect of output price uncertainty on investment for the entire sample, but they do find a negative uncertainty effect for the more competitive industries. More specifically, their benchmark estimation results show that for the most competitive sample, the estimated elasticity of output uncertainty is -0.116, indicating that a 10 per cent increase in output price uncertainty should induce a 1.16 per cent decrease in the rate of investment. On the other hand, for the noncompetitive industry (60 per cent), the estimated elasticity of output price uncertainty is not significant. This result is robust over both alternative measurements of price uncertainty and other control variables. This again suggests that the degree of competition in product markets is one of the factors that influence the effect of output price uncertainty. It is interesting to notice that an unambiguous conclusion on the relationship between product market competition and uncertainty effects on investment cannot be drawn from these two studies. In the former a lower degree of competition is associated with a greater negative demand uncertainty effect, whereas in the latter a lower degree of competition is associated with a smaller negative price uncertainty effect on investment. Again, other factors such as the source of uncertainty or the risk attitude of the firm may be a significant additional force that influences the investment-uncertainty relationship.

6.3.4   Substitutability of Production Factors

There are few empirical studies which investigate the investment-uncertainty relationship by considering the impact of the substitutability of production factors. An exception is Guiso and Parigi (1999) who test this hypothesis using Italian firm-level survey data. By regressing the demand for labour hours on expected demand and the constructed demand uncertainty measure, and controlling for other variables, they find that higher uncertainty decreases the demand for labour. Based on the assumption that capital and labour are complementary, they conclude that high demand uncertainty discourages capital investment. This result of course does not prove complementarity. It may be the case that over the business cycle underutilization of capital takes place, which could interfere with the direct complementarity between capital and labour. On the other hand there may also be a labour hoarding effect.

Leahy and Whited (1996) also test the impact of the factor substitutability between labour and capital on the investment–uncertainty relationship. They use two indicators to proxy for the degree of the substitutability between labour and capital: (1) the variance of the labour-capital ratio, and (2) the level of the labour-capital ratio. The higher the variance (or the level) of the labour-capital ratio, the more variable the labour-capital ratio is and hence the higher the ability to substitute labour for capital may be. It should be noted that differences in variance may be due to different degrees of utilization of capital and labour. Leahy and Whited first divide the entire sample on the basis of the median of the labour-capital ratio of the industry. The results show a greater negative uncertainty effect for the group of firms with a higher ability to substitute labour for capital. The explanation is that firms will choose technologies with variable capital-labour ratios if they find uncertainty particularly costly. This explanation may be somewhat artificial since there may be other important factors, like real wages and returns to scale that influence these decisions.

6.4 CONCLUSIONS

This chapter reviews empirical research on the investment-uncertainty relationship. We focus on practical issues, such as how to measure uncertainty, what the evidence of the investment uncertainty relationship is, and what the factors are that influence the investment uncertainty relation. The methods used to construct uncertainty measures of random variables in the empirical investment literature are many. There is no consensus on the performance of different uncertainty measures in investment equations. The choice of methods to operationalize uncertainty appears to be mainly based on data availability.

Empirical evidence suggests that uncertainty almost always has a negative effect on investment. The irreversibility property of investment aggravates the negative uncertainty effect on investment. Other factors that influence the investment-uncertainty relationship are: financial constraints faced by the firm, the degree of competition in product markets, the substitutability of production factors, and the source of uncertainty.

PART THREE

Conclusion

7. Conclusions

This book presented an overview of both theory and empirics of the relationship between investment, financial imperfections and uncertainty. Traditionally, there are two fields that are studied separately:

- Investment and capital market imperfections;
- Investment under uncertainty.

Both fields may provide a better understanding of the empirics of investment. The literature on empirical investment still has large problems in explaining observed investment behaviour. Especially on the firm level it seems hard to identify the key determinants of physical investment. Fifteen years ago, the empirical investment literature seemed to be in a slump. Since the late 1980s both lines of literature provided new hope.

In this book we gave an overview of the two fields and their empirical results. We first reviewed the capital market imperfections literature and the empirical results. Next, we discussed both traditional investment models with uncertainty and the more modern options based models. In the latter models the timing of investment is crucial. We presented a review of the empirics of the modelling of investment under uncertainty.

A theoretical synthesis between the two lines of literature seems natural but is rather difficult to make. Starting from the literature of capital market imperfections one could include the option to wait in a net present value analysis of firm investment. Suppose that a firm faces an interest rate on a loan that is too high. This can be caused by asymmetric information between the bank and the firm on the quality of the investment project. The firm may still invest in a later period if some of the uncertainty is resolved and the hurdle to invest is lowered. These models get rather complicated however and are rather difficult to use in empirical work.

One could also start from the investment under uncertainty literature and include financial imperfections. Starting from the Dixit-Pindyck model using contingent claim analysis would not be natural, since this model assumes a perfect spanning of financial markets. This implies that the valuation of the option is based on financial market perfection. The hope for theoretical progress is rather limited.

This is the main reason why we concentrated on empirical support of the importance of the relationship between investment, uncertainty and imperfections of financial markets. We showed some applications of various techniques to model uncertainty and to include these measures into investment models. We can draw the following general conclusions from this:

1.   There exists an overwhelming empirical support of the negative sign of the investment-uncertainty relationship. This evidence coincides with the general belief but contradicts the textbook case of perfect competition on the goods market and risk neutral firms. The evidence shown is robust across various assumptions regarding uncertainty measures, degrees of irreversibility and the theoretical investment model.

2.   The type of uncertainty is found to be rather unimportant. Obviously one could argue that demand or output price uncertainty has an impact that is unequal to cost uncertainty. In the empirical results we do not find any indication that this distinction disturbs the sign of the relationship.

3.   The studies shown illustrate that the financial situation of the firm interacts with uncertainty. Especially the leverage of the firm is important in this respect. Here we can observe that high debt can signal two things: (1) financial distress, and (2) the ability to attract external funds. For some firms more inflationary uncertainty might be profitable since it erodes the real debt. For others the high interest rates may lead to too high interest payments which may lead to serious distress.

On the agenda for further research we would like to put the following list of topics:

- A better, perhaps continuous, measurement of uncertainty *ex ante* (a continuous survey of firms). This may help our understanding of the changes in risk facing the firm.

- An improvement of the measurement of reversibility of investment in physical capital. What are the prices of second-hand capital goods?

- Theoretical models of financial imperfections and uncertainty. For instance the dividend decision of the firm could be modelled simultaneously with the investment under uncertainty decision.

- It would also be interesting to study early abandonment of investment projects through changes in uncertainty. This could help understanding asymmetries in buying and selling capital goods.

- The development of models and testable hypothesis on the appropriateness of various combinations of assumptions on the key determinants of the sign of the investment uncertainty relationship. At the moment we can only test joint hypotheses without precisely knowing the relevance for the structural assumptions. This leads to the problem of estimating the deep structural parameters of investment models.

- More empirical work on the unlisted firms is wanted. Usually listed firms are popular because of the availability of databases (*Compustat, Global Vantage*). But smaller firms are responsible for the big changes in employment; therefore it is important to collect more data for nonlisted firms.

- The nonlinearity of the investment-uncertainty relation seems to be a promising field of research.

PART FOUR

Appendices

A. Derivation of the q and Euler Model

This appendix shows how the q model and the Euler approach can be derived from a general model. It starts with the maximization problem of the firm:

$$V_t = E[\sum_{j=0}^{\infty} \beta_{t+j} \Pi_{t+j} | \Omega_t] \qquad (A.1)$$

where V_t represents the expected present value of cash flows, $E[.|\Omega_t]$ is the conditional expectation based on information set Ω_t, β_{t+j} is the discount factor between t and $t+j$ and Π_{t+j} represent net cash flow. One can conceive of V_t as the stock market valuation of the firm. Define:

$$\beta_{t+j} = \Pi_{i=1}^{j}(1+r_{t+i})^{-1} \qquad (A.2)$$

where r_{t+i} is the nominal discount rate between $t+i-1$ and $t+i$. Net cash flow is given by:

$$\Pi_t = p_t[F(K_t,L_t) - G(I_t,K_t)] - w_t L_t - p_t^I I_t \qquad (A.3)$$

with K_t the capital stock, L_t a vector of costlessly adjustable factors, I_t investment, p_t price of output, p_t^I the price of investment, w_t the price vector of L_t, $F(.,.)$ the production function, and $G(.,.)$ the adjustment cost function. By definition, capital accumulation follows:

$$K_t = (1-\delta)K_{t-1} + I_t \qquad (A.4)$$

where δ represents the depreciation rate.

The maximization problem to be solved can now be rewritten as:

$$V_t(K_{t-1}) = \max \Pi(K_t,L_t,I_t) + E[\beta_{t+1}V_{t+1}(K_t)|\Omega_t] \qquad (A.5)$$

The solution is:

$$\frac{\partial V_t}{\partial K_{t-1}} = -(1-\delta)\frac{\partial \Pi_t}{\partial I_t} \tag{A.6}$$

$$\frac{\partial \Pi_t}{\partial L_t} = 0 \tag{A.7}$$

The shadow value of capital along the optimal path is given by:

$$\frac{\partial V_t}{\partial K_{t-1}} = (1-\delta)\frac{\partial \Pi_t}{\partial K_t} + (1-\delta)E[\beta_{t+1}\frac{\partial V_{t+1}}{\partial K_t}|\Omega_t] \tag{A.8}$$

The problem in this class of models is that the shadow value of capital is unobservable. Two of these solutions are the q approach and the Euler approach.

A.1   THE q MODEL

In the q approach q represents the ratio of the market value of capital to the replacement value of capital and can be related to the unobservable shadow value of capital. The firm is supposed to be a price taker in all markets. Equation (A.3) can be differentiated with respect to the control variable investment (I_t) and the single state variable capital (K_t), in order to obtain:

$$\left(\frac{\partial \Pi}{\partial I}\right)_t = -p_t\left(\frac{\partial G}{\partial I}\right)_t - p_t^I \tag{A.9}$$

$$\left(\frac{\partial \Pi}{\partial K}\right)_t = p_t\left[\left(\frac{\partial F}{\partial K}\right)_t - \left(\frac{\partial G}{\partial K}\right)_t\right] \tag{A.10}$$

Combining these with Condition (A.6) yields:

$$\left(\frac{\partial G}{\partial I}\right)_t = \left(\frac{\lambda_t}{p_t^I} - 1\right)\frac{p_t^I}{p_t} \tag{A.11}$$

In this condition:

$$\lambda_t = \frac{V_t/K_{t-1}}{1-\delta} \tag{A.12}$$

is the shadow value of one extra unit of capital. Tobin's q is defined as $q_t = \lambda_t/p_t^I$. q_t is marginal q and includes all future expected net revenues. Hayashi (1982) has shown that average and marginal q are related if both the production function $F(.)$ and the adjustment cost function $G(.)$ are homogeneous of degree one in the production factors K and L. This facilitates the empirical use of average q. Despite this shortcut, the empirics of q are problematic as stock market data do not give a unique representation (*e.g.* Perfect and Wiles, 1994).

A.2 THE EULER MODEL

The Euler approach starts with Conditions (A.8) and (A.6). Substitution of (A.12) into (A.8) yields:

$$\lambda_t = \left(\frac{\partial \Pi}{\partial K} \right)_t + (1 - \delta) E [\beta_{t+1} \lambda_{t+1} | \Omega_t] \qquad (A.13)$$

We can derive:

$$(1 - \delta) E \left[\beta_{t+1} \left(\frac{\partial \Pi}{\partial I} \right)_{t+1} | \Omega_t \right] = \left(\frac{\partial \Pi}{\partial I} \right)_t + \left(\frac{\partial \Pi}{\partial K} \right)_t \qquad (A.14)$$

This is the basic Euler condition. The Euler equation approach to modelling investment has some disadvantages, however. As Chirinko (1993, p. 1894) argues this approach uses limited information to maximize just one corporate goal. As compared to the q model, the Euler model faces an alternative problem, namely the specification of marginal productivity of capital.

B. Utility Functions and Assumptions Regarding Risk

B.1 UTILITY FUNCTIONS AND RISK

This section presents the various types of utility functions normally used and their implications for risk behaviour. Usually, it is assumed that a firm's attitude towards risk can be represented by a Von Neumann-Morgenstern utility function. Such a utility function satisfies several conditions. The first is that there is nonsatiation, which means that more is preferred over less. Mathematically, this implies a positive first derivative. With a Von Neumann-Morgenstern utility function risk aversion corresponds to a strictly concave function or, in other words, a utility function with a negative second derivative. Risk loving implies a convex utility function: a utility function with a positive second derivative. Finally, risk neutrality corresponds to a linear utility function, *i.e.* a utility function with a second derivative of zero. Summarizing:

- $U''(\Pi) < 0$: a concave utility function, which implies risk averse behaviour;
- $U''(\Pi) > 0$: a convex utility function, which implies risk loving behaviour; and
- $U''(\Pi) = 0$: a linear utility function, which implies risk neutral behaviour.

The next question is how preferences change when the level of wealth increases, assuming a utility function in wealth. There are three possibilities:

1. decreasing absolute risk aversion, which implies that an increase in wealth leads investors to increase their level of investment in risky assets;

2. constant absolute risk aversion - the level of investment in risky assets stays the same although wealth increases; and

3. increasing absolute risk aversion - the level of investment in risky assets increase when wealth increases.

It can be shown that the form of absolute risk aversion depends on the so-called Arrow-Pratt measure of absolute risk aversion, defined as:

$$A(W) = \frac{-U''(W)}{U'(W)} \qquad (B.1)$$

where

- $A'(W) > 0$: increasing absolute risk aversion;
- $A'(W) = 0$: constant absolute risk aversion; and
- $A'(W) < 0$: decreasing absolute risk aversion.

Another question is how the percentage of wealth invested in risky assets changes when wealth increases. This can be measured by the Arrow-Pratt coefficient of relative risk aversion, which is defined as:

$$R(W) = \frac{-WU''(W)}{U'(W)} = WA(W) \qquad (B.2)$$

$R'(W) > 0$ implies increasing relative risk aversion, which in turn implies that the percentage of wealth invested in risky assets declines when wealth increases; $R'(W) = 0$ implies constant relative risk aversion and $R'(W) < 0$ implies decreasing relative risk aversion.

The best known types of utility functions that imply risk averse behaviour are:

1. constant relative risk aversion utility functions:

$$U(\Pi) = \frac{\Pi^{1-\alpha}}{1-\alpha} \qquad (B.3)$$

with $\alpha > 0$ and $\alpha \neq 1$, or:

$$U(\Pi) = \log(\Pi) \qquad (B.4)$$

2. constant absolute risk aversion utility functions or exponential utility functions:

$$U(\Pi) = -\frac{1}{\alpha}e^{-\alpha c} \qquad (B.5)$$

3. linear quadratic utility function:

$$U(\Pi) = \Pi - \frac{a}{2}\Pi^2 \qquad (B.6)$$

where $(1 - a\Pi) > 0$ in order to satisfy the condition of nonsatiation. It is easy to show that this function displays increasing absolute and relative risk aversion. The advantage of a linear quadratic utility function is that expected utility can be written in terms of means and variances as follows. The variance of a random variable is:

$$\sigma_{\Pi}^2 = E[\Pi - E[\Pi]]^2 \qquad (B.7)$$

so that.

$$\sigma_{\Pi}^2 = E[\Pi^2] - E[\Pi]^2 \qquad (B.8)$$

For a linear quadratic function, the expected value can be written as:

$$E[U(\Pi)] = E[\Pi] - \frac{a}{2}E[\Pi^2] \qquad (B.9)$$

By substituting (B.8) into (B.9) one obtains:

$$E[U(\Pi)] = E[\Pi] - \frac{a}{2}(\sigma_{\Pi}^2 + E[\Pi]^2) \qquad (B.10)$$

B.2 MEAN PRESERVING SPREAD AND JENSEN'S INEQUALITY

Many analyses compare the effect of uncertainty with the certainty outcome. Hence, they give the *overall* impact of uncertainty. A different issue concerns the *marginal* impact, *i.e.* the effect of slightly more risk on firm behaviour. Unfortunately, it is not clear how this can be done. Most authors try to apply the mean preserving spread concept of Rothschild and Stiglitz (1970). Because of its importance, we elaborate on this concept.

A mean preserving spread is obtained by adding a random variable with conditional mean zero to the original random variable. The effects of increased uncertainty are then examined by replacing the original random variable p by a new random variable $p + z$, where $E[z] = 0$. By using Jensen's inequality it can be derived that the expected value of a convex (concave) function increases (decreases) as its argument undergoes a mean preserving spread (see *e.g.* Hartman, 1972, 1976).

Formally, Jensen's inequality states that if x is a random variable and $f(x)$

is a convex function of x, then:

$$E[f(x)] > f(E[x]) \tag{B.11}$$

This implies that in the case where the expected value of x remains the same but the variance of x increases, $E[f(x)]$ increases. The following example may explain matters. Consider the convex function $f(x) = x^2$ and assume that x is a random variable that may take the values 0,1 and 2. It can now be calculated that $E[x] = 1$, that $f(E[x]) = 1$ and that $E[f(x)] = 5/3$. Now assume that the stochastic variable x may take the values -1, 1, 3. Now $E[x] = 1$, $f(E[x]) = 1$ and $E(f[x]) = 11/3$. Hence, the expected value of a convex function increases when a stochastic variable is replaced by a new stochastic variable with the same mean but with higher variance.

Alternatively, the expected value of a concave function of a random variable x is lower than the expected value of a concave function of a new random variable z with the same mean but a lower variance than x. Hence, for a concave function $E[f(x)] \leq E(f[z])$. The mean preserving spread concept of risk means that a random variable x is more risky than a random variable z if for all concave functions f, $E[f(x)] \leq E[f(z)]$. Since a concave function corresponds to risk averse behaviour, this concept implies that a random variable x is riskier than a random variable z whenever a risk averse investor would prefer the random return z to the random return x.

C. Ito's Lemma and Dynamic Programming

C.1 WIENER PROCESSES AND ITO'S LEMMA

In many economic models it is assumed that a stochastic process can be described by a Wiener process. In this section we give a deliberately brief explanation of a Wiener process. A Wiener process is not differentiable in the conventional way. Since in practice we often work with functions of different generalizations of Wiener processes which we would like to differentiate, we also explain the method used to differentiate a Wiener process, the so-called Ito's lemma.

This section is very much based on Chapter 3 of Dixit and Pindyck (1994) and Chapter 8 of Ferguson and Lim (1998). The reader is referred to these books and to the references in these books for more detailed descriptions of stochastic processes.

The Wiener process, also called Brownian motion, is a continuous time limit of a discrete time random walk model, which is given by:

$$x_t = x_{t-1} + z_t \tag{C.1}$$

where z is a normally distributed random variable with mean zero and independent increments. A Wiener process is a useful specification of a stochastic process when there is a continuous stream of random walk type shocks. If there is only a single shock with timing unknown, the process is better described by a Poisson process. For reasons of space, however, we do not deal with Poisson processes.

The random walk model, and therefore also the Wiener process, satisfies the Markov property, meaning that the mathematical expectation of the value of x at period t depends only on its value at $t-1$, since this value incorporates all information of the past values of x. The random walk model also satisfies the Martingale property which implies that the best prediction of the value of x_{t+1} is the value x_t.

More formally, a Wiener process has the following properties. If z_t is a

Wiener process then:

1.   the relationship between dz and dt is given by: $dz = \varepsilon \sqrt{dt}$, where ε is a normally distributed random variable with a mean of zero and a standard deviation of 1. Since the random variable has a mean of zero and a standard deviation of 1, $E(dz) = 0$ and $Var(dz) = E(dz)^2 = dt$. Hence, the variance increases with time, so that the Wiener process is nonstationary;

2.   the random variable ε_t is serially uncorrelated. Hence $E(\varepsilon_t, \varepsilon_s) = 0$.

A Wiener process can be easily generalized in a broad class of stochastic processes in continues time, so-called Ito processes. Well known examples are Brownian motion with drift, *i.e.* $dx = \alpha dt + \sigma dz$, and geometric Brownian motion, *i.e.* $dx = \alpha x dt + \sigma x dz$, where in both cases dz is an increment of a Wiener process as described above. α and σ are the drift and variance parameters, respectively.

A Wiener process cannot be differentiated in the conventional way since the derivative with respect to time does not exist (dz/dt gives a term of order $o(\sqrt{dt})/o(dt) \to \infty$ as dt goes to zero). For this reason Ito's lemma should be used. Ito's lemma is a tool used to differentiate and integrate functions of Ito processes. In order to apply Ito's lemma, the rules of multiplication for Wiener terms have to be known. Letting z_i and z_j be Wiener terms these results are:

$$dz = 0 \tag{C.2}$$
$$(dt)^2 = 0 \tag{C.3}$$
$$(dz_i)^2 = dt \tag{C.4}$$
$$(dz_i)(dz_j) = \rho_{ij}dt \tag{C.5}$$
$$(dz_i)(dt) = 0 \tag{C.6}$$

where ρ_{ij} is the correlation between two Wiener processes. Consider the function $F(x,t)$ and assume that x_t follows a Brownian motion with drift:

$$dx = fdt + \sigma dz \tag{C.7}$$

where dz is the increment of a Wiener process and f and σ are nonrandom constants. What is the total differential of $F(x,t)$? In normal cases it would be:

$$dF = \frac{\partial F}{\partial x}dx + \frac{\partial F}{\partial t}dt \tag{C.8}$$

However, since a Wiener process does not have a time derivative in the conventional sense, we have to apply Ito's lemma. Ito's lemma uses a second order Taylor expansion of $F(x,t)$. This gives:

$$dF = \frac{\partial F}{\partial x}dx + \frac{\partial F}{\partial t}dt + \frac{1}{2}\frac{\partial^2 F}{\partial x^2}(dx)^2 + \frac{1}{2}\frac{\partial^2 F}{\partial x^2}(dt)^2 + \frac{\partial^2 F}{\partial x \partial t}(dx)(dt) \quad (C.9)$$

Since $(dt)^2 = 0$ (see above), and $(dx)(dt) = [fdt + \sigma dz]dt = f(dt)^2 + \sigma dzdt = 0$, dF equals:

$$dF = \frac{\partial F}{\partial x}dx + \frac{\partial F}{\partial t}dt + \frac{1}{2}\frac{\partial^2 F}{\partial x^2}(dx)^2 = F_x dx + F_t dt + \frac{1}{2}F_{xx}(dx)^2 \quad (C.10)$$

The last term normally goes to zero when dt becomes infinitesimal and therefore is not taken into account. With Ito processes, however, this is not the case. Substituting the stochastic differential equation the result becomes:

$$dF = F_x[fdt + \sigma dz] + F_t dt + \frac{1}{2}F_{xx}[fdt + \sigma dz]^2 \quad (C.11)$$

which can be rewritten as:

$$
\begin{aligned}
dF &= [F_x f + F_t]dt + \sigma F_x dz + \frac{1}{2}F_{xx}(f^2(dt)^2 + \sigma^2(dz)^2 + 2f\sigma dt dz) \\
&= [F_x f + F_t + 0.5F_{xx}\sigma^2]dt + \sigma F_x dz \quad (C.12)
\end{aligned}
$$

C.2   DYNAMIC PROGRAMMING

There are three major approaches to solving dynamic optimization problems: the calculus of variation, optimal control theory, and dynamic programming. We certainly do not intend to give a detailed explanation of any of these approaches. The interested reader is referred to one of the many available textbooks on dynamic optimisation. However, since most authors who solve dynamic investment problems under uncertainty use the Dynamic Programming approach, we provide a brief explanation of this method. [1]

The fundamental idea of Dynamic Programming is to rewrite a multi-period dynamic optimization problem in a series of simpler two period optimization problems. Basically, the sequence of decisions is divided into two parts: the immediate period, and the remaining decisions which are summarized in the continuation value. The optimal solution is then found by working backwards: we start at the end of the planning period. Since there is no future at the end of the planning period, the problem is basically a one period static problem and it is easy to find the best choice and the continuation value. We can now go to the decision period preceding the last period, and solve the current period, which is again a static problem since we know the expected continuation value. This procedure is repeated until the first decision period. Although this basic idea is very simple, in practice the solution of continuous-time Dynamic Programming problems is often difficult since it involves the use of partial differential equations.

Cho (1997) gives a simple two period example of how dynamic programming works. For reasons of convenience we present a slightly altered version here. An economic agent optimizes utility over two periods. It maximizes:

$$U(k_1, c_1) + \frac{1}{1+\rho} E[U(k_2, c_2)] \qquad (C.13)$$

subject to $k_2 = f(k_1, c_1)$, where k is the quantity of capital goods (the state variable), c is consumption (control variable), ρ is the discount rate and E denotes expectation. This problem is solved in five steps.

1. Solve the problem for the last period. Maximize $\frac{1}{1+\rho} U(k_2, c_2)$ with respect to c_2 and obtain an optimum decision function for c_2 as a function of k_2, i.e.:

$$\frac{\partial U(k_2, c_2)}{\partial c_2} = 0 \Rightarrow c_2 = g(k_2) \qquad (C.14)$$

2. Set up the value function for the second period $V_2(k_2)$, i.e.:

$$V_2(k_2) = U(k_2, g(k_2)) \qquad (C.15)$$

3. Form an objective function for the two period problem:

$$U(k_1, c_1) + \frac{1}{1+\rho} U(k_2, c_2) = U(k_1, c_2) + \frac{1}{1+\rho} E[V_2(k_2)] \qquad (C.16)$$

4. Substitute the dynamic constraint for k_2 in the objective function:

$$U(k_1, c_1) + \frac{1}{1+\rho} E[V_2(f(k_1, c_1))] \qquad (C.17)$$

5. Maximize the objective function with respect to c_1 and obtain an optimum decision function for c_1 as a function of x_1:

$$\frac{\partial U(k_1, c_1)}{\partial c_1} + \frac{1}{1+\rho} E\left[\frac{\partial f(k_1, c_1)}{\partial c_1} \frac{\partial V_2}{\partial k_2}\right] = 0 \Rightarrow c_1 = g_1(k_1) \qquad (C.18)$$

The value function for the first period can now be written as:

$$V_1(k_1) = U(k_1, g_1(k_1)) + \frac{1}{1+\rho} E[V_2(k_2)] \tag{C.19}$$

The entire process can be summarized in the so-called Bellman equation:

$$V_1(k_1) = \max_{c_1} \left[U(k_1, c_1) + \frac{1}{1+\rho} E[V_2(k_2)] \right] \tag{C.20}$$

The subscripts 1 and 2 are replaced by t and $t+1$, respectively, when the problem involves more than two periods. If the problem refers to an infinite horizon problem, we cannot work backwards from a known final value function. However, we can still use the recursive structure of the problem. If the utility function and discount rate are independent of the actual date, the value functions become independent of time for infinite horizon problems (the value function converges to some function $V(k_t)$), therefore:

$$V(k_t) = \max_{c_t} \left[U(k_t, c_t) + \frac{1}{1+\rho} E[V(k_{t+1})] \right] \tag{C.21}$$

We proceed by considering the continuous time problem. If each time period is of length Δt and when ρ is the discount rate per unit time, the Bellman equation becomes:

$$V(k_t) = \max_{c_t} \left[U(k_t, c_t)\Delta t + \frac{1}{1+\rho\Delta t} E[V(k_{t+\Delta t})] \right] \tag{C.22}$$

By multiplying with $1 + \rho\Delta t$ and some rewriting, one obtains:

$$\begin{aligned} \rho\Delta t V(k_t) &= \max_{c_t} [U(k_t, c_t)\Delta t(1 + \rho\Delta t) + E[V(k_{t+\Delta t}) - V(k_t)]] \\ &= \max_{c_t} [U(k_t, c_t)\Delta t(1 + \rho\Delta t) + E[\Delta V]] \end{aligned} \tag{C.23}$$

Dividing by Δt gives:

$$\rho V(k_t) = \max_{c_t} \left[U(k_t, c_t)(1 + \rho\Delta t) + \frac{1}{\Delta t} E[\Delta V] \right] \tag{C.24}$$

Taking the limit of Δt (which goes to zero) gives:

$$\rho V(k_t) = \max_{c_t} \left[U(k_t, c_t) + \frac{1}{dt} E[dV] \right] \tag{C.25}$$

This is the form of the Bellman equation we often see in dynamic investment models with uncertainty. The left hand side gives the required return per unit of time for the decision maker. The right hand side gives the immediate pay-out (dividend) plus the expected rate of capital gain (see Dixit and Pindyck, 1994, p. 105). Optimality requires that the expected return equals the required return. Since V is already a maximum value function, we can rewrite the above equation as:

$$\rho V(k_t)dt = \max_{c_t} U(k_t, c_t)dt + E[dV] \qquad (C.26)$$

This equation is sometimes also presented as:

$$0 = \max_{c_t} U(k_t, c_t)e^{-\rho t}dt + E[dJ] \qquad (C.27)$$

The difference reduces to the method of discounting. In the latter case, al-though the decision period (the lower bound in the integral for a multi period optimization problem) starts at t, the value function is evaluated at period 0. In the former case, the value function is evaluated at period t (hence $J = Ve^{-\rho t}$).

Before ending this Appendix we briefly consider a class of a dynamic pro-gramming problem which is especially relevant for the option approach to in-vestment: the optimal stopping problem. In an optimal stopping problem there is a binary choice in each period. The firm decides to wait one more period, or decides to invest. Investing means "stopping", whereas waiting corresponds to "continuing". In this case the Bellman equation is formulated as:

$$F(x_t) = \max\left(\Omega(x_t), \pi(x_t) + \frac{1}{1+\rho}E[F(x_{t+1})]\right) \qquad (C.28)$$

where $\Omega(x_t)$ is the termination payoff and $\pi(x_t) + \frac{1}{1+\rho}E[F(x_{t+1})]$ the continu-ation payoff. In most investment models continuation (waiting) does not give any immediate profit flow, so that the Bellman equation becomes:

$$F(x_t) = \max\left(\Omega(x_t), \frac{1}{1+\rho}E[F(x_{t+1})]\right) \qquad (C.29)$$

For most economic applications it is possible to find a critical level of x^* that divides the range of possible values of x into two areas: termination on one side is optimal, whereas continuation on the other side is optimal. Under certain conditions we can derive a curve $x = x^*(t)$ that divides the space into a continuation and a termination area.

The next step is to consider the Bellman equation in the continuation region. To this end, consider only the second term on the right hand side of equation

(C.28) or (C.29), depending on whether there is an immediate profit flow in the continuation regime. In continuous time these equations can be rewritten as:

$$\rho F(x_t) = \max \left[\pi(x_t) + \frac{1}{dt} E[dF] \right] \tag{C.30}$$

or:

$$\rho F(x_t) = \frac{1}{dt} E[dF] \tag{C.31}$$

In order to find a solution and the threshold, we must consider some boundary conditions at $x = x^*$. The boundary conditions commonly used are the "value-matching" and the "smooth-pasting" conditions. The "value-matching" condition is derived as follows: in the stopping regime $F(x_t) = \Omega(x_t)$, so that for a continuous function it must hold that:

$$F(x_t^*, t) = \Omega(x_t^*, t), \tag{C.32}$$

The value-matching condition equilibrates the unknown value function with the known termination payoff function. The smooth-pasting condition requires that $F(x_t)$ and $\Omega(x_t)$ are tangent at x_t^*, hence:

$$F_x(x_t^*, t) = \Omega_x(x_t^*, t) \tag{C.33}$$

NOTES

1. According to Cho (1997) many problems that are usually solved by using the Dynamic Programming approach are much more easily solved by using the Lagrange method.

Bibliography

Abel, A.B. (1983), 'Optimal investment under uncertainty', *The American Economic Review*, **72**, 228–233.

Abel, A.B., A.K. Dixit, J.C. Eberly and R.S. Pindyck (1996), 'Options, the value of capital, and investment', *Quarterly Journal of Economics*, **111**, 753–777.

Abel, A.B. and J.C. Eberly (1994), 'A unified model of investment under uncertainty', *The American Economic Review*, **84**, 1369–1384.

Abel, A.B. and J.C. Eberly (1996), 'Optimal investment with costly reversibility', *Review of Economic Studies*, **63**, 581–593.

Abel, A.B. and J.C. Eberly (1999), 'The effects of irreversibility and uncertainty on capital accumulation', *Journal of Monetary Economics*, **44**, 339–377.

Abel, A.B. and O.J. Blanchard (1986), 'The present value of profits and cyclical movements in investment', *Econometrica*, **54**, 249–273.

Aizenman, J. and N.P. Marion (1993), 'Macroeconomic uncertainty and private investment', *Economics Letters*, **41**, 207–210.

Aizenman, J. and N.P. Marion (1999), 'Volatility and investment: interpreting from developing countries', *Economica*, **66**, 157–179.

Akerlof, G. (1970), 'The market for lemons: qualitative uncertainty and the market mechanism', *Quarterly Journal of Economics*, **84**, 488–500.

Alonso-Borrego, C. and S. Bentolila (1994), 'Investment and *q* in Spanish manufacturing', *Oxford Bulletin of Economics and Statistics*, **56**, 49–55.

Arrow, K.J. (1968), 'Optimal capital policy with irreversible investment', in J.N. Wolfe (ed.), *Value, Capital and Growth, Essays in Honour of Sir John Hicks*: Edinburgh University Press.

Atiyas, I. (1992), 'Financial reform and investment behaviour in Korea: evidence from panel data', Paper prepared for the conference on the impact of financial reform: World Bank.

Audretsch, D.B. and J.A. Elston (1994), 'Does firm size matter? Evidence on the impact of liquidity constraints on firm investment behaviour in Germany', CEPR Discussion Paper 1072: Center for Economic Policy Research.

Barnett, S.A. and P. Sakellaris (1999), 'A new look at firm market value, investment and adjustment costs', *The Review of Economics and Statistics*,

81, 250–260.

Barran, F. and M. Peeters (1996), 'Internal finance and corporate investment: Belgian evidence with panel data', Working paper: Université Catholique de Louvain.

Bell, G.K. and J.M. Campa (1997), 'Irreversible investments and volatility markets: A study of the chemical processing industry', *The Review of Economics and Statistics*, **79**, 79–87.

Berger, A.N. and G.F. Udell (1995), 'relationship lending and lines of credit in small firm finance', *Journal of Business*, **68**, 351–381.

Bernanke, B.S. (1983), 'Irreversibility, uncertainty, and cyclical investment', *Quarterly Journal of Economics*, **98**, 85–106.

Bertola, G. (1998), 'Irreversible investment', *Research in Economics*, **52**, 3–37.

Bester, H. (1985), 'Screening versus rationing in credit markets with imperfect information', *The American Economic Review*, **75**, 850–855.

Bhattacharya, S. (1979), 'Imperfect information, dividend policy, and the 'Bird in the Hand' fallacy', *Bell Journal of Economics*, **10**, 259–270.

Blanchard, O.J., F. Lopez de Silanes and A. Shleifer (1994), 'What do firms do with cash windfalls?', *Journal of Financial Economics*, **36**, 337–360.

Blundell, R., S.R. Bond, M.P Devereux and F. Schiantarelli (1992), 'Does q matter for investment? Some evidence from a panel of U.K. companies', *Journal of Econometrics*, **51**, 233–257.

Bo, H. (1999a), 'Investment and uncertainty: a survey of the empirical literature', Mimeo: University of Groningen.

Bo, H. (1999b), 'The q theory of investment: Does uncertainty matter?', SOM Research Report 99E07: University of Groningen.

Bond, S., J.A. Elston, J. Mairesse and B. Mulkay (1994), 'A comparison of empirical investment equations using company panel data for France, Germany, Belgium and the UK', Mimeograph: Institute for Fiscal Studies.

Bond, S.R. and C. Meghir (1994), 'Dynamic investment models and the firm's financial policy', *Review of Economic Studies*, **61**, 197–222.

Boyd, J.H. and E.C. Prescott (1986), 'Financial intermediary-coalitions', *Journal of Economic Theory*, **38**, 211–232.

Brennan, M. and A. Kraus (1987), 'Efficient financing under asymmetric information', *The Journal of Finance*, **42**, 1225–1243.

Butters, J.K. and J.V. Lintner (1945), *The effect of federal taxes on growing enterprises*: Harvard University, Graduate School of Business Administration.

Caballero, R.J. (1991), 'On the sign of the investment-uncertainty relationship', *The American Economic Review*, **81**, 279–288.

Caballero, R.J. and J. Leahy (1996), 'Fixed costs: The demise of marginal Q', NBER Working Paper Series 5508: NBER.

Caballero, R.J. and R.S. Pindyck (1996), 'Uncertainty, investment, and industry revolution', *International Economic Review*, **37**, 641–662.

Calem, P.S. and J.A. Rizzo (1994), 'Financing constraints and investment: new evidence from hospital industry data', Working paper: Federal Reserve Bank.

Calomiris, C.W. and C.P. Himmelberg (1995), 'Investment banking costs as a measure of the cost of access to external finance', Mimeograph: Columbia University.

Calomiris, C.W. and R.G. Hubbard (1995), 'Internal finance and investment: evidence from the undistributed profits tax of 1936-1937', *The Journal of Business*, **68**, 443–482.

Carpenter, R.E. (1992), 'The effect of liquidity on firm financial constraints', PhD thesis: Washington University.

Carpenter, R.E., S.M. Fazzari and B.C. Petersen (1994), 'Inventory investment, internal finance fluctutations, and the business cycle', *Brookings Papers on Economic Activity*, pp. 75–138.

Chapman, R., B. Junior and T. Stegman (1994), 'Cash flow constraints and firms' investment behaviour', *Applied Economics*, **28**, 1037–1044.

Chatelain, J-B. (1996), 'Investment facing an endogenous debt ceiling: an explicit model', Mimeo: Banque de France.

Chiang, A.C. (1992), *Elements of Dynamic Optimization*: McGraw-Hill.

Chirinko, R.S. (1993), 'Business fixed investment spending: modeling strategies, empirical results, and policy implications', *Journal of Economic Literature*, **31**, 1875–1911.

Chirinko, R.S. (1996), 'Finance constraints, liquidity, and investment spending: cross-country evidence', Mimeograph: Emory University.

Chirinko, R.S. and H. Schaller (1995), 'Why does liquidity matter in investment equations?', *Journal of Money, Credit, and Banking*, **27**, 527–548.

Chow, G.C. (1997), *Dynamic Economics: Optimization by the Lagrange Method*: Oxford University Press.

Clark, P.K. (1979), 'Investment in the 1970s: theory, perfromance and prediction', *Brookings Papers on Economic Activity*, **1979:1**, 73–113.

Constantinides, G.M. and B.D. Grundy (1989), 'Optimal investment with stock repurchase and financing as signals', *The Review of Financial Studies*, **2**, 445–466.

Corbett, J. and T. Jenkinson (1997), 'How is investment financed? A study of Germany, Japan, the United Kingdom and the United States', *The Manchester School, Supplement*, **25**, 69–93.

Das, S.P. (1980), 'Further results on input choices under uncertain demand', *The American Economic Review*, **70**, 528–532.

De Meza, D. and D.C. Webb (1987), 'Too much investment in problems of asymmetric information', *Quarterly Journal of Economics*, **102**, 179–222.

Deloof, M. (1996), 'Internal capital markets, bank borrowing, and financing constraints: evidence from Belgian firms', Mimeo: Free University of Brussels.

Devereux, M. and F. Schiantarelli (1990), 'Investment, financial factors and cash flow: evidence from UK panel data', in R.G. Hubbard (ed.), *Asymmetric information, corporate finance and investment*: University of Chicago Press, pp. 279–306.

Diamond, D.W. (1989), 'Reputation acquisition in debt markets', *Journal of Political Economy*, **97**, 828–862.

Diamond, D.W. and O.H. Dybvig (1983), 'Bank runs, deposit insurance and liquidity', *American Economic Review*, **55**, 1126–1150.

Dickens, W.T. and K. Lang (1985), 'A test of dual labor market theory', *The American Economic Review*, **75**, 792–805.

Dixit, A.K. and R.S. Pindyck (1994), *Investment under uncertainty*: Princeton University Press.

Duessenberry, J.S. (1958), *Business cycles and economic growth*: McGraw-Hill.

Ees, H. van and J.H. Garretsen (1994), 'Does liquidity matter for business investment? some evidence for the Netherlands', *Journal of Macroeconomics*, **16**, 613–627.

Ees, H. van, J.H. Garretsen, L. de Haan and E. Sterken (1998), 'Investment and debt constraints: evidence from Dutch panel data', in S. Brakman, H. van Ees and S.K. Kuipers (eds), *Market Behaviour and Macroeconomic Modelling*: MacMillan, Chapter 6, pp. 159–179.

Eisner, R. (1978), *Factors in business investment*: Ballinger Press.

Eisner, R. and R.J. Strotz (1963), 'Determinants of business investment', in Commission on Money and Credit (eds), *Impacts of Monetary Policy*: Prentice-Hall, pp. 59–233.

Elston, J.A. (1996), 'Investment, liquidity constraints and bank relationships: Evidence from German manufacturing firms', Discussion Paper Series 1329: CEPR.

Elston, J.A. and H. Albach (1994), 'Bank affiliations and firm capital investment in Germany', Working paper: Wissenschaftszentrum.

Episcopos, A. (1995), 'Evidence on the relationship between uncertainty and irreversible investment', *The Quarterly Review of Economics and Finance*, **35**, 41–52.

Estrada, A. and J. Vallés (1995), 'Investment and financial costs: Spanish evidence with panel data', Servicio de Estudios Documento de Trabajo 9506: Banco de España.

Fama, E.F. and M.H. Miller (1972), *The theory of finance*: Holt, Rinehart, and Winston.

Fazzari, S.M., R.G. Hubbard and B.C. Petersen (1988a), 'Financing constraints and corporate investment', *Brookings Papers on Economic Activity*, pp. 141–195.

Fazzari, S.M., R.G. Hubbard and B.C. Petersen (1988b), 'Investment, financing decisions, and tax policy', *The American Economic Review*, **78**, 200–205.

Fazzari, S.M., R.G. Hubbard and B.C. Petersen (1993), 'Working capital and fixed investment: new evidence on financing constraints', *RAND Journal of Economics*, **24**, 328–341.

Ferderer, J. P. (1993a), 'The impact of uncertainty on aggregate investment spending: An empirical analysis', *Journal of Money, Credit, and Banking*, **25**, 3–48.

Ferderer, J. P. (1993b), 'Does uncertainty affect investment spending?', *Journal of Post-Keynesian Economics*, **16**, 19–35.

Ferguson, B.S. and G.C. Lim (1998), *Introduction to dynamic economic models*: Manchester University Press.

Fisher, I. (1911), *The purchasing power of money*: MacMillan.

Fisher, I. (1930), *Theory of interest*: MacMillan.

Fohlin, C. (1998), 'Relationship banking, liquidity, and investment in the German industrialization', *The Journal of Finance*, **53**, 1737–1758.

Frisse, K., M. Funke and F. Lankes (1993), 'An empirical analysis of West-German corporate investment decisions using company-level panel data', *Zeitschrift für Wirtschafts- und Sozialwissenschaften*, **113**, 579–595.

Gale, D. and M. Hellwig (1985), 'Incentive compatible debt contracts: the one period problem', *Review of Economic Studies*, **52**, 647–663.

Galeotti, M., F. Schiantarelli and F. Jaramillo (1994), 'Investment decisions and the role of debt, liquid assets and cash flow: evidence from Italian panel data', *Applied Financial Economics*, **4**, 121–132.

Gertler, M. and S. Gilchrist (1994), 'Monetary policy, business cycles and the behaviour of small manufacturing firms', *Quarterly Journal of Economics*, **109**, 309–340.

Gertler, M., R.G. Hubbard and A.K. Kashyap (1991), 'Interest rate spreads, credit constraints, and market fluctuations: an empirical investigation', in R.G. Hubbard (ed.), *Financial markets and financial crises*: University of Chicago Press, pp. 1–31.

Ghosal, V. (1991), 'Demand uncertainty and the capital-labor ratio: evidence from the U.S. manufactoring sector', *The Review of Economics and Statistics*, **73**, 157–160.

Ghosal, V. (1995), 'Input choices under price uncertainty', *Economic Inquiry*, **33**, 142–158.

Ghosal, V. and P. Loungani (1996), 'Product market competition and the impact of price uncertainty on investment: some evidence from US manufacturing industries', *Journal of Industrial Economics*, **44**, 217–228.

Ghosal, V. and P. Loungani (2000), 'The differential impact of uncertainty on investment in small and large businesses', *The Review of Economics and Statistics*, **82**, 338–349.

Gilchrist, S. (1990), 'An empirical analysis of corporate investment and financing hierarchies using firm level panel data', Mimeo: Board of Governors of the Federal Reserve System.

Gilchrist, S. and C.P. Himmelberg (1995), 'Evidence on the role of cash-flow in reduced-form investment equations', *Journal of Monetary Economics*, **36**, 541–572.

Gilchrist, S. and E. Zakrajcek (1995a), 'Investment and the present value of profits: an analysis using firm level QFR data', Mimeograph: Boston University.

Gilchrist, S. and E. Zakrajcek (1995b), 'The importance of credit for macroeconomic activity: identification through heterogeneity', Mimeograph: Boston University.

Greenwald, B., J.E. Stiglitz and A. Weiss (1984), 'Information imperfections in the capital market and macroeconomic fluctuations', *The American Economic Review, Papers and Proceedings*, **74**, 194–199.

Gross, D. (1994), 'The investment and financing decisions of liquidity constrained firms', Mimeograph: Massachussets Institute of Technology.

Grossman, S. and O. Hart (1979), 'A theory of competitive equilibrium in stock market economies', *Econometrica*, **47**, 293–330.

Guariglia, A. (1997), 'The effects of financial constraints on inventory investment: evidence from a panel of UK firms', Mimeo: University of Essex.

Guiso, L. and G. Parigi (1999), 'Investment and demand uncertainty', *Quarterly Journal of Economics*, **114**, 185–227.

Hall, B.H. (1991), 'R&D investment at the firm level: does the source of financing matter?', Working paper series: National Bureau of Economic Research.

Hamermesh, D.S. and G.A. Pfann (1996), 'Adjustment costs in factor demand', *Journal of Economic Literature*, **34**, 1264–1292.

Hansen, B.E. (1999), 'Threshold effects in non-dynamic panels: estimation, testing, and inference', *Journal of Econometrics*, **93**, 345–368.

Harris, J.R., F. Schiantarelli and M.G. Siregar (1994), 'The effect of financial liberalization on the capital structure and investment decisions of Indonesian manufacturing establishments', *World Bank Economic Review*, **8**, 17–47.

Harris, M. and A. Raviv (1990), 'Capital structure and the informational role of debt', *The Journal of Finance*, **45**, 321–349.

Harris, M. and A. Raviv (1991), 'The theory of capital structure', *Journal of Finance*, **46**, 297–355.

Hart, O. (1995), *Firms, contracts, and financial structure*: Oxford University Press.

Hartman, R. (1972), 'The effect of price and cost uncertainty on investment', *Journal of Economic Theory*, **5**, 258–266.

Hartman, R. (1976), 'Factor demand with output price uncertainty', *The Amer-*

ican Economic Review, **66**, 675–681.

Hayashi, F. (1982), 'Tobin's marginal q and average q: a neoclassical interpretation', *Econometrica*, **50**, 213–224.

Hermes, N. and R. Lensink (1998a), 'Regulatory change and the allocation of finance: the role of business conglomerates in chili, 1983-1992', in V. Murinde Doukas, J. and C. Wihlborg (eds), *Financial sector reform and privatization in transition economies*: North Holland, pp. 217–239.

Hermes, N. and R. Lensink (1998b), 'Banking reform and the financing of firm investment: an empirical analysis of the chilean experience, 1983-1992', *The Journal of Development Studies*, **34**, 27–43.

Himmelberg, C.P. (1990), 'Essays on the relationship between investment and internal finance', PhD thesis: Northwestern University.

Himmelberg, C.P. (1991), 'A dynamic analysis of dividend and investment behaviour under borrowing constraints', Mimeograph: New York University.

Himmelberg, C.P. and B. Petersen (1994), 'R and D and internal finance: a panel study of small firms in high-tech industries', *Review of Economics and Statistics*, **76**, 38–51.

Hirshleifer, D. and A. Thakor (1989), 'Managerial reputation, project choice and debt', Working Paper 14-89: Anderson Graduate School of Management at UCLA.

Holthausen, D.M. (1976), 'Input choices and uncertain demand', *The American Economic Review*, **66**, 94–103.

Hoshi, T., A.K. Kashyap and D. Scharfstein (1991), 'Corporate structure, liquidity, and investment: evidence from Japanese industrial groups', *Quarterly Journal of Economics*, **106**, 33–60.

Hsiao, C. and A.K. Tahmiscioglu (1996), 'A panel analysis of liquidity constraints and firm investment', Mimeo: University of Southern California.

Hu, X. and F. Schiantarelli (1998), 'Investment and capital market imperfections: a switching regression approach using firm panel data', *The Review of Economics and Statistics*, **53**, 466–479.

Hubbard, R.G. (1998), 'Capital market imperfections and investment', *Journal of Economic Literature*, **36**, 193–225.

Hubbard, R.G., A.K. Kashyap and T.M. Whited (1995), 'Internal finance and firm investment', *Journal of Money, Credit, and Banking*, **27**, 683–701.

Hubbard, R.G. and A.K. Kashyap (1992), 'Internal net worth and the investment process: an application of U.S. agriculture', *Journal of Political Economy*, **100**, 506–534.

Huizinga, J. (1993), 'Inflation uncertainty, relative price uncertainty, and investment in U.S. manufacturing', *Journal of Money, Credit, and Banking*, **25**, 521–527.

Jaffee, D. and T. Russell (1976), 'Imperfect information, uncertainty, and credit rationing', *Quarterly Journal of Economics*, **81**, 651–666.

Jaramillo, F., F. Schiantarelli and A. Weiss (1996), 'Capital market imperfections, financial constraints and investment: econometric evidence from panel data for Ecuador', *Journal of Development Economics*, **51**, 367–386.

Jensen, M.C. (1986), 'Agency cost of free cash flow, corporate finance and takeovers', *The American Economic Review, Papers and Proceedings*, **76**, 323–329.

Jensen, M.C. and W.R. Meckling (1976), 'Theory of the firm: managerial behavior, agency costs, and ownership structure', *Journal of Financial Economics*, **3**, 305–360.

Jorgenson, D.W. (1963), 'Capital theory and investment behavior', *The American Economic Review*, **53**, 247–259.

Jorgenson, D.W. (1971), 'Econometric studies of investment behaviour', *Journal of Economic Literature*, **9**, 1111–1147.

Kadapakkam, P.R., P.C. Kumar and L.A. Riddick (1998), 'The impact of cash flows and firm size on investment: the international evidence', *Journal of Banking and Finance*, **22**, 293–320.

Kahneman, D. and A. Tversky (1979), 'Prospect theory: an analysis of decision under risk', *Econometrica*, **47**, 263–291.

Kaplan, S.N. and L. Zingales (1997), 'Do investment-cash flow sensitivities provide useful measures of financing constraints?', *Quarterly Journal of Economics*, **112**, 169–215.

Kashyap, A.K. and J.C. Stein (1994), 'Monetary policy and bank lending', in N.G. Mankiw (ed.), *Monetary Policy*: University of Chicago for the National Bureau of Economic Research.

Keeton, W. (1979), *Equilibrium credit rationing*: Garland Press.

Keynes, J.M. (1936), *The general theory of employment, interest and money*: MacMillan.

Kwan, E. (1994), 'The role of financial constraints on the firm's investment: evidence from the retail trade sector', Mimeo: New York University.

Lamont, O. (1997), 'Cash flow and investment: evidence from internal markets', *The Journal of Finance*, **52**, 83–109.

Leahy, J. and T.M. Whited (1996), 'The effects of uncertainty on investment: some stylized facts', *Journal of Money, Credit, and Banking*, **28**, 64–83.

Leland, H.E. (1972), 'Theory of the firm facing uncertain demand', *The American Economic Review*, **62**, 278–291.

Leland, H.E. and D.H. Pyle (1977), 'Informational asymmetries, financial structure and financial intermediation', *The Journal of Finance*, **32**, 371–387.

Lensink, R. and E. Sterken (2001), 'The option to wait to invest and equilibrium credit rationing', *Journal of Money, Credit, and Banking*, **33**, forthcoming.

Lyon, A. (1992), 'Taxation, information asymmetries, and a firm's financing choices', Policy Research Working Paper 936: World Bank.

Magill, M. and M. Quinzii (1996), *Theory of incomplete markets*: MIT Press.

Mattesini, F. (1993), *Financial markets, asymmetric informatiomn and macroeconomic equilibrium*: Dartmouth.

McDonald, R. and D. Siegel (1986), 'The value of waiting to invest', *Quarterly Journal of Economics*, **101**, 707–728.

McKenna, C.J. (1986), *The economics of uncertainty*: Wheatsheaf Books.

Meyer, J.R. and E. Kuh (1957), *The investment decision: an empirical study*: Harvard University Press.

Meyer, J.R. and R.R. Glauber (1964), *Investment decisions, economic forecasting, and public policy*: Harvard University, Graduate School of Business Administration.

Modigliani, F (1982), 'Debt, dividend policy, taxes, inflation and market valuation', *The Journal of Finance*, **37**, 255–273.

Modigliani, F (1988), 'Mm-past, present, future', *Journal of Economic Perspectives*, **4**, 149–158.

Modigliani, F. and M.H. Miller (1958), 'The cost of capital, corporate finance, and the theory of investment', *The American Economic Review*, **48**, 178–197.

Modigliani, F. and M.H. Miller (1963), 'Corporate income taxes and the cost of capital: a correction', *The American Economic Review*, **53**, 443–444.

Moret, Ernst and Young (1996), *Ondernemend vermogen in perspectief (in Dutch)*: Moret, Ernst and Young.

Myers, S.C. (1982), 'The capital structure puzzle', *Journal of Finance*, **39**, 575–592.

Myers, S.C. and S. Majluf (1984), 'Corporate financing decisions when firms have investment information that investors do not', *Journal of Financial Economics*, **13**, 187–220.

Ng, S. and H. Schaller (1993), 'The risky spread, investment and monetary policy transmission: evidence on the role of asymmetric information', Mimeo: Carleton University.

Nickell, S.J. (1978), *The investment decision of firms*: Cambridge University Press.

Noe, T. (1988), 'Capital structure and signalling game equilibria', *The Review of Financial Studies*, **1**, 331–356.

Oliner, S.D. and G.D. Rudebusch (1992), 'Sources of financing hierarchy for business investment', *Review of Economics and Statistics*, **74**, 643–654.

Pagan, A. and A. Ullah (1988), 'The econometric analysis of models with risk terms', *Journal of Applied Econometrics*, **3**, 87–105.

Pattillo, C. (1998), 'Investment, uncertainty, and irreversibility in Ghana', *IMF Staff Papers*, **45**, 522–553.

Peeters, M. (1997), 'Does demand and price uncertainty affect Belgian and Spanish corporate investment?', Staff paper: De Nederlandsche Bank.

Perfect, S.B. and K.W. Wiles (1994), 'Alternative constructions of Tobin's Q: an empirical comparison', *Journal of Empirical Finance*, **1**, 313–341.

Petersen, M.A. and R.G. Rajan (1994), 'The benefits of firm-creditor relationships: evidence from small business data', *Journal of Finance*, **49**, 3–38.

Pfann, G.A. and B. Verspagen (1989), 'The structure of adjustment costs for labour in the Dutch manufacturing sector', *Economics Letters*, **29**, 365–371.

Pindyck, R.S. (1982), 'Adjustment costs, uncertainty and the behaviour of the firm', *The American Economic Review*, **72**, 415–427.

Pindyck, R.S. (1986), 'Capital risk and models of investment behaviour', Working Paper 1819: MIT SLoan School of Management.

Pindyck, R.S. (1991), 'Irreversibility, uncertainty, and investment', *Journal of Economic Literature*, **29**, 1110–1148.

Pindyck, R.S. (1993), 'A note on competitive investment under uncertainty', *The American Economic Review*, **83**, 273–277.

Pindyck, R.S. and A. Solimano (1993), 'Economic instability and aggregate investment', Policy Research Working Paper 1148: The World Bank.

Price, S. (1995), 'Aggregate uncertainty, capacity utilizaton and manufacturing investment', *Applied Economics*, **27**, 147–154.

Price, S. (1996), 'Aggregate uncertainty, investment and asymmetric adjustment in the U.K. manufacturing sector', *Applied Economics*, **28**, 1369–1379.

Rajan, R.G. and L. Zingales (1996), 'What do we know about capital structure?', *The Journal of Finance*, **50**, 1421–1460.

Riley, J.D. (1987), 'Credit rationing: a further remark', *The American Economic Review*, **77**, 224–227.

Rondi, L., A. Sembenelli and G. Zanetti (1994), 'Is excess sensitivity of investment to financial factors constant across forms? Evidence from panel data on Italian companies', *Journal of Empirical Finance*, **1**, 365–383.

Rothschild, M. and J.E. Stiglitz (1970), 'Increasing risk: 1. a definition', *Journal of Economic Theory*, **2**, 225–243.

Sandmo, A. (1971), 'On the theory of the competitive firm under price uncertainty', *The American Economic Review*, **61**, 65–73.

Sarkar, S. (2000), 'On the investment-uncertainty relationship in a real options model', *Journal of Economic Dynamics and Control*, **24**, 219–225.

Scaramozzino, P. (1997), 'Investment irreversibility and finance constraint', *Oxford Bulletin of Economics and Statistics*, **59**, 89–108.

Schaller, H. (1993), 'Asymmetric information, liquidity constraints, and Canadian investment', *Canadian Journal of Economics*, **26**, 552–574.

Schiantarelli, F. and A. Sembenelli (1995), 'Form of ownership and financing constraints: panel data evidence from leverage and investment equations', Working Paper 286: Boston College.

Serven, L. (1997), 'Uncertainty, instability, and irreversible investment', Policy Research Working Paper 1722: The World Bank.

Shin, H.H. and R.M. Stulz (1998), 'Are internal capital markets efficient', *Quarterly Journal of Economics*, **93**, 531–552.

Siregar, M.G. (1995), *Indonesia's financial liberalization: an empirical analysis of 1981-1988 panel data*: Institute of Southeast Asian Studies.

Stevens, G.V.G (1974), 'On the impact of uncertainty on the value and investment of the neoclassical firm', *The American Economic Review*, **64**, 319–336.

Stiglitz, J.E. (1969), 'A re-examination of the Modigliani-Miller theorem', *The American Economic Review*, **59**, 784–793.

Stiglitz, J.E. and A. Weiss (1981), 'Credit rationing in markets with imperfect information', *The American Economic Review*, **71**, 393–410.

Stiglitz, J.F. and A. Weiss (1983), 'Incentive effects of terminations: applications to the credit and labor markets', *The American Economic Review*, **73**, 912–927.

Stiglitz, J.E. and A. Weiss (1987), 'Credit rationing: Reply', *The American Economic Review*, **77**, 228–231.

Stulz, R. (1990), 'Managerial discretion and optimal financing policies', *Journal of Financial Economics*, **26**, 3–27.

Summers, L.H. (1981), 'Taxation and corporate investment: a q-theory approach', *Brookings Papers on Economic Activity*, pp. 67–127.

Tinbergen, J. (1939), 'A method and its application to investment theory', in *Statistical testing in business cycle theories*, Vol. 1: League of Nations.

Tobin, J. (1969), 'A general equilibrium approach to monetary theory', *Journal of Money, Credit, and Banking*, **1**, 15–29.

Trigeorgis, L. (1996), *Real Options; Managerial Flexibility and Strategy in Resource Allocation*: MIT Press.

Vogt, S.C. (1994), 'The cash flow/investment relationship: evidence from U.S. manufacturing firms', *Financial Management*, **23**, 3–20.

Wald, J. (1995), 'How firm characteristics affect capital structure: an international comparison', Working paper: University of California.

Whited, T.M. (1992), 'Debt, liquidity constraints, and corporate investment: evidence from panel data', *Journal of Finance*, **47**, 1425–1460.

Whited, T.M. (1995), 'Why and to what extent do Euler equations fail?', Working paper: University of Delaware.

Williamson, S.D. (1986), 'Costly monitoring, financial intermediation and equilibrium credit rationing', *Journal of Monetary Economics*, **18**, 159–179.

Williamson, S.D. (1987), 'Costly monitoring, loan contracts and equilibrium credit rationing', *Quarterly Journal of Economics*, **102**, 135–146.

Zakrajcek, E. (1994), 'Retail inventories, internal finance, and aggregate fluctuations: evidence from firm-level panel data', Mimeograph: New York University.

Zakrajcek, E. (1995), 'Econometric analysis of real and financial decisions using firm-level Quarterly Financial Report QFR data', PhD thesis: New York University.

Zeira, J. (1990), 'Cost uncertainty and the rate of investment', *Journal of Economic Dynamics and Control*, **14**, 53–63.

Author Index

Subject Index

Uncertainty, 7
Underinvestment, 16, 24, 26
Underpricing, 24
Unit root test, 103
Universal banking, 36, 40
User cost of capital, 1, 33, 61, 78
Utility function, 57, 125–127, 133

Value matching condition, 81
Value of assets in place concept, 82
Value of the firm, 7, 8, 13, 23–25, 44, 68, 72, 80

VAR model, 2, 31, 46
Volatility, 101–104, 107, 109
Von Neumann-Morgenstern utility function, 125

Walrasian prices, 15
Wedge, 2, 27–29, 37, 44, 63, 79, 82, 83
Wiener process, 67, 68, 79, 80, 84, 101, 103, 129, 130